Rebecca Probert is widely recognised as the leading authority on the history of the marriage laws of England and Wales, a subject on which she has written extensively. Currently Professor of Law at the University of Warwick, she read law at St Anne's College, Oxford, took her LLM at University College, London, worked as a researcher at the Law Commission, and has lectured in family law since 1997. She has spent many years deeply engrossed in the large-scale genealogical case-studies which underpin the conclusions of her academic work and of this book. Her many TV and radio appearances include *Who Do You Think You Are?*, *Heirhunters*, *Great Houses with Julian Fellowes*, and *Harlots, Heroines & Housewives*. In 2015 she acted as a specialist advisor to the Law Commission on its scoping paper *Getting Married*.

Professor Probert is constantly adding to her body of research on the history of marriage and its application to genealogy, and would love to hear from family historians on any of the many topics raised in this book. Details of how to get in touch are on p. 159.

Also by Rebecca Probert

Divorced, Bigamist, Bereaved? (Takeaway, 2015)

Marriage Rites & Rights (Hart, 2015), co-edited with Miles and Mody

The Changing Legal Regulation of Cohabitation: From Fornicators to Family, 1600 to 2011 (Cambridge University Press, 2012)

Cretney & Probert's Family Law (Sweet & Maxwell, 8th ed., 2012)

The Rights & Wrongs of Royal Marriage (Takeaway, 2011)

'Cogently argued, eminently readable... the ideal family lawyer's stocking filler'

Marriage Law and Practice in the Long Eighteenth Century: A Reassessment (Cambridge University Press, 2009)

'The word "groundbreaking" is, for once, an accurate description.... Professor Probert comprehensively trashes the work of many scholars (including some of great eminence) who have written about marriage and the family—indeed some of them might think they should hand back their honorary degrees and many more will breathe sighs of relief that research funding once granted cannot in practice be reclaimed.'

International Journal of Law in Context

'Every so often comes along a book which challenges long-established orthodoxies; this is one such publication.... The arguments advanced are... both convincing and compelling.'

Ecclesiastical Law Journal

MARRIAGE LAW
FOR
GENEALOGISTS

The Definitive Guide

...what everyone tracing their family history
needs to know about
where, when, who and how
their English and Welsh ancestors married

revised second edition

Rebecca Probert

TAKEAWAY

This edition first published in Great Britain in 2016
by Takeaway (Publishing)

2nd edition, v. 1.0 LS

Copyright © Rebecca Probert 2016

Rebecca Probert has asserted her right to be identified as the author of this work

Takeaway (Publishing), 33 New Street, Kenilworth CV8 2EY

E-mail: books@takeawaypublishing.co.uk

British Library Cataloguing in Publication Data.
A catalogue record for this book is available from the British Library

ISBN 978-0-9931896-2-3

For Dad,
who first introduced me
to Lord Hardwicke's Act

TABLE OF CONTENTS

WHY DO GENEALOGISTS NEED A GUIDE TO MARRIAGE LAW?

INTRODUCTION
THE APPROACH OF THIS BOOK
KEY DEFINITIONS OF LEGAL TERMS
HOW THE LAW OF MARRIAGE WORKS
COMMON MISTAKES

INTRODUCTION

I was in my early teens when my father decided to start researching our family tree. We spent many hours in Warwickshire Record Office, patiently reading through parish registers. Conveniently—if somewhat disappointingly for one hoping for evidence of some scandalous forbears—our ancestors proved remarkably easy to find, with each preceding generation appearing in the marriage registers at neatly spaced intervals.

When I later came to read accounts of marriage law and practice in earlier centuries this conformity seemed all the more surprising: many scholars seemed to be claiming that informal marriages had been common before Lord Hardwicke's Clandestine Marriages Act of 1753, and that even after it had come into force many couples preferred to cohabit rather than comply with its provisions. One respected historian even went so far as to suggest that before 1754 half the population married in a simple folk ceremony!

Were this true, then family historians might well despair of finding their ancestors in the parish registers, or assume a particular virtue on the part of those they did find. Many may, like myself, have begun to doubt claims about the informality of marriage in earlier centuries.

Such doubts led me, a decade and a half ago, to set out to investigate the original case-law, statutes, legal treatises, and other literature, and to begin researching other people's ancestors—analysing the data for entire communities and cohorts, spending weeks at a time in public record offices the length and breadth of England and Wales, and countless more scouring databases to piece together the lives and loves of many thousands of individuals through marriage registers and censuses.

The results of this research were published in a number of academic articles and monographs and overturned many long-standing myths about how our ancestors married. The simple but very clear findings are that the overwhelming majority of couples married in the Church of England, cohabitation was vanishingly rare, and informal marriage practices non-existent. Realising that these findings would have very practical implications for those tracing their family tree, I wrote *Marriage Law for Genealogists* to provide a short and simple but nonetheless definitive guide to the marriage law of England and Wales over the last four centuries, focusing on the sorts of questions that genealogists encounter.

In the four years since its first publication, I have spoken to many thousands of family historians and responded to many queries about puzzling marriages. The questions that related to second (or subsequent) marriages inspired a second book, *Divorced, Bigamist, Bereaved?* This dealt in much more depth with remarriage after divorce or death (and the more problematic remarriages that were preceded by neither!); it also dealt with the situation where the same two people remarried one another (which happened much more often than one might think).

In the meantime, my own work on marriage law has continued, and this second edition of *Marriage Law for Genealogists* includes some new case-studies and examples, including points raised by questions I have received from family historians. It also brings the law on various points up to date, since there have been significant changes over the past few years to who can marry whom, and when, and how.

The approach of this book

The starting point of 1600 was chosen partly for convenience (relatively few family historians will succeed in tracing their ancestors back to before this date) and partly because there are a cluster of legal developments in the first years of the seventeenth century that form a useful starting point when discussing the law (the decision of the Star Chamber in 1602 that remarriage following an official separation was not possible; legislation dealing with bigamy in 1603; and the canons of 1604, setting out the Church's requirements on marriage, all of which are discussed later at pp. 46, 55 and 75). The focus will be on the position in the eighteenth, nineteenth and early twentieth centuries, since this is the period of most interest to family historians. Developments in the later decades of the twentieth century are sketched out where this is necessary to bring a particular story up to date; those who are interested in pursuing them further can find all the information in a modern family law textbook.

The book is limited to the law of England and Wales. This has been substantially one and the same since the sixteenth century, and is generally known for reasons of brevity as 'English law'. (The use of 'English' to mean both English and Welsh in this book is not intended in any way as a slight upon the beautiful nation of Wales, in which the author has spent much time teaching and travelling, and which is, besides, the ultimate home of her family surname.) Scotland, by contrast, has always had its own distinct laws of marriage and is referred to only tangentially (when, for example, we come to look at the infamous phenomenon of Gretna Green elopements). Similarly, Ireland (both the North and the Republic) has its own complex legal history which is beyond the scope of this book. The legal treatment by the law of England and Wales of those who travelled abroad and married *beyond* these shores is discussed in the final chapter.

Writers always hope that their readers will peruse every word that they have carefully penned. The reality, of course, is that every reader has their own agenda. In particular, those tracing their family tree may have very specific questions about particular types of marriages, rather than wanting an overview of marriage law in its entirety. For this reason, this book is structured around key questions, rather than simply describing each piece of legislation in turn.

WHETHER & WHY deals with the likelihood of any given couple having gone through a valid ceremony of marriage.

WHO examines *who* could marry (in terms of mental capacity and being free to marry) and *whom* they could and could not marry (focusing on the prohibited degrees and how these changed over time).

How then looks at the basic formalities required for a valid marriage from 1600 to the present day, and how Catholics, Protestant dissenters and others married at any given time.

WHEN turns to the age at which couples married, looking at the minimum age at which it was possible to marry as well as when it was possible to marry without parental consent. This chapter also provides evidence on the average age at marriage across the period, and on the stage in a couple's relationship at which marriage occurred. It also discusses the seasons, days, and hours when marriages could be, and were, celebrated.

WHERE moves beyond the legal requirements (since the parish in which a marriage is celebrated has never affected its validity) and draws on large-scale studies to provide guidance to the family historian on where they may need to look for the marriages of their ancestors.

Where these issues overlap (for example, the question of *when* a couple may need parental consent in order to marry also requires knowledge of *how* it was possible to marry), the reader is directed to the relevant pages.

DEFINITIONS OF KEY LEGAL TERMS

Certain key legal concepts, by contrast, run through this book like the letters in a stick of Brighton rock, and they are set out here for ease of reference.

Valid

A valid marriage is one that is recognised as a marriage by every court, and for all legal purposes. Any children born after the marriage are legitimate, and the marriage can only be ended by death or divorce.

Clandestine

Before 1754, a clandestine marriage was simply one celebrated by an Anglican clergyman that failed to comply with *all* of the requirements of the canon law. There was not necessarily any secrecy or wrongdoing involved, and such a marriage was perfectly valid. The only adverse consequence was that the parties could be punished by the church courts for not observing the canon law. After 1754, however, the term 'clandestine' became associated with secret elopements (e.g. in Garrick and Coleman's 1766 play *The Clandestine Marriage*), and many later historians have been misled into assuming that all clandestine marriages were of this kind.

Voidable

A voidable marriage is one that may be annulled by a court but which is regarded as valid unless and until a decree of nullity is issued. It cannot be challenged after the death of either of the parties. However, before 1971 a decree of nullity operated retrospectively, so that the marriage was declared to have been void from the start, thus bastardizing any children of the union.

Void

A void marriage is regarded by the law as never having existed. It is void from the start without any formal annulment by a court. However, it must be remembered that:

(i) the presumption of the law is that a marriage is valid, and so the onus is on the person challenging a marriage to show that it is void. Very clear evidence is required to satisfy a court that a marriage is void. Where the challenge is that the formalities were not properly observed, it is particularly difficult to establish this, especially if a significant period of time has elapsed.

(ii) while nothing that the parties later do can change a void marriage into a valid one, legislation may retrospectively validate marriages that would have been void at the time they were celebrated.

There are a variety of ways to describe how a court may deal with a void or voidable marriage: it can 'avoid' it (i.e., make it void), invalidate it, annul the marriage, declare it to be void, declare that it never existed, declare it to be invalid, or issue a decree of nullity. All of these are the same, and are equally correct.

There are two terms I have avoided using: the word *illegal* has unfortunate and potentially misleading connotations of criminality; if a particular marriage would have exposed the parties to sanctions under the criminal law (for example in cases of bigamy), I have stated this explicitly. The term *irregular* is equally problematic, as different meanings have been ascribed to it by different historians; it does not, however, have any technical legal meaning.

The above definitions may conflict with what family historians have read elsewhere. Rather than asking readers to take it on trust that this account is correct, this introductory chapter will first set out some of the common mistakes and misunderstandings that bedevil the other works in this area.

HOW THE LAW OF MARRIAGE WORKS

The subtitle of one popular book aimed at family historians asks the question *Was Your Ancestor Really Married?*, and its authors expend a great deal of effort attempting to show that our ancestors were, for various reasons, not technically married in the eyes of the law. Suffice it to say here that such arguments, though written with the best intentions, are rendered meaningless by a basic failure to grasp how the law of marriage actually works.

How the law aims for certainty

The law has as its goal *certainty* over people's marital status. For all manner of legal and social reasons, individuals and society have always needed to know for sure whether or not a couple were validly married. To achieve this, the law has always set out certain formal requirements, yet a slavish insistence on the black-and-white letter of the law can actually *reduce* certainty by questioning a marriage's validity on purely technical grounds. Rather than being the inflexible regime that is often portrayed, the law of marriage in England and Wales has across the centuries been accommodating toward unintentional mistakes yet strict toward fraud and deception. It is both complex but instinctive, subtle but precise, a fine balance of pragmatism and idealism.

The distinction between 'mandatory' and 'directory'

This can be illustrated by the basic distinction that exists in English law between requirements that are 'mandatory' and those that are merely 'directory'. These concepts are vital to understanding the law. If a particular requirement is mandatory, then a failure to comply with it renders the marriage void. If, though, it is only directory, then the marriage will still be valid even if it is ignored. In other words, the law sets up a framework to channel marriages into a standard form, in the interests of legal certainty, but makes a pragmatic and sensible distinction between those aspects of the ceremony that are vital to the very existence of a marriage and those that, while desirable, are not fundamental.

For writers of genealogical guides who are unaware of this basic distinction, the fact that a statute set out a particular requirement is taken as proof that it was essential to the validity of a marriage. This mistake is so common that it would be unjust to single out any particular writer; to take just one example, family historians are often told that if a statute required pages to be numbered or lined in a certain way in a marriage register, the marriage could be void if such details were not followed. But a moment's reflection should make any reader realise the unlikelihood of any rational system invalidating a marriage, bastardizing any offspring, and jeopardizing the inheritance of property, just because the page on which it was recorded was not numbered. And in fact, when we look at the detailed provisions of the Marriage Act 1753 with a lawyer's eye we can see that such minutiae were only directory: it did not matter how, or even *whether*, a marriage was registered (see p. 83). Those writing without the benefit of training in eighteenth-century statutory interpretation cannot be expected to know that their conclusions are wrong, yet they are wrong nonetheless.

> **Key fact: there is a basic distinction in the law of marriage between requirements that are mandatory (essential to validity) and directory (not essential to validity).**

This is not to suggest that directory requirements were of no effect. Far from it. As this book will show, even directory requirements had a dramatic impact on actual practice, but their impact was achieved by other means. Punishing clergymen for failing to observe the law often ensured that everything was done correctly. And at a more basic level, there has always been a basic tendency to observe the 'rules of the game': an engaged couple, told that weddings could only take place between 8 a.m. and 6 p.m. (as was the case until October, 2012), would duly arrange for it to take place within those hours, rather than ask what would happen if they got married a bit later. The very existence of rules has always encouraged conformity, even if (as in this example) the marriage would still have been legally valid if it took place at 6.05 p.m (see further p. 133).

How the law redresses its own mistakes

Of course, the law does not always get it right. Litigation exposes loopholes and oversights that require Parliament to confirm the status of certain marriages. By way of a simple example, legislation had to be passed to validate marriages celebrated in churches and chapels built after the 1753 Act was passed (see p. 82), as legislators had failed to phrase the legislation in a way that would include them. As a result, marriages which would have been void at the time they were celebrated became valid. A more dramatic example is that of a marriage to one's late wife's sister: for most of the nineteenth century such marriages were void (see p. 63), but legislation in 1907 not only allowed them to go ahead but also retrospectively validated those that had already taken place.

Key fact: in deciding whether a marriage is valid, we need to
ask ourselves not only what its status was at the time it was
celebrated, but also what its status is now.

Some people might be troubled to find that a marriage that was
void one day can be valid the next; the law, by contrast, tends to be
pragmatic on such matters and performs these sleights of hand in
the interests of certainty and fairness. The impression of inflexibility
which many historians like to depict when writing about marriage
law is undeserved.

How the law prefers to presume that a marriage is valid

Another way in which the law promotes certainty over marital status
is by making certain presumptions. These legal presumptions have
been as much misunderstood by lawyers without an understanding
of history as they have been by historians who are not legally trained.
If a couple have gone through a ceremony of marriage, lived together
as husband and wife, and are reputed to be validly married, then
the legal presumption is that the ceremony was properly performed
and that their marriage is valid. If questions are later raised over its
validity, the onus is on the person challenging it to show that it was
not properly performed. In other words, the presumption of English
law is always in favour of validity.

Key fact: English law has always placed the onus on the person
challenging a marriage to show that it is invalid, rather than
on the person wanting to prove its validity to show that it was
properly performed.

This is vital for the family historian, researching events that took
place many decades or even centuries ago. The fact that at certain
periods it was mandatory for a marriage to be preceded by banns or
licence does not mean that a marriage should be assumed to be void
if there is no evidence of the banns being called or a licence obtained.

The relevance of cohabitation and reputation

The reason why 'cohabitation and repute' is relevant in establishing a presumption in favour of the validity of the ceremony is because this could be important evidence of what was known about the marriage at the time. Its role can be seen more clearly if we think about the alternatives. If a couple separated immediately after the ceremony and never set up home together, might this perhaps suggest that they knew the marriage was never valid? Or if a couple went through a ceremony and *did* set up home together, but the rumour in the neighbourhood was that they were not married, this might hint at local knowledge of some flaw in the proceedings or a suspicion that the couple were not free to marry each other.

Dealing with cases where there is no evidence of a ceremony

The same is true of the presumption that operated where no evidence of a ceremony was to be found. While the parties to the marriage were alive, they might be able to provide testimony of where the wedding had taken place. But if the validity of the marriage was challenged at a later date, perhaps in a dispute over inheritance, their descendants might well have no idea where or when it had taken place.

Even if these details were remembered, it was entirely possible that no documentary evidence existed and that the clergyman who had celebrated it had died. All an individual might be able to show was that everyone had always *thought* that their forebears were validly married.

The law, working on the basis that couples were highly unlikely to set up home together and be regarded by the community as married unless this was actually the case, regarded such evidence of cohabitation and repute as sufficient to raise a presumption that there had been a valid marriage. This did not necessarily establish that there had been a marriage—the person challenging its existence might in turn provide evidence that there had always been doubts as to the validity of the marriage, and it was then was for the judge to decide who had the more convincing case. The challenges—familiar to any family historian—of proving the specific details of an ancestor's marriage were thus mitigated in practice by sensible presumptions that took into account the difficulties created by time and chance.

Marriage 'by cohabitation and repute'?

It is important to stress that a marriage could not be *created* by a couple setting up home together and holding themselves out as married. There is also no justification for the claim made by many historians that couples simply cohabited in the belief that the law would eventually regard them as married. For one thing, this mistakenly assumes that the community would simply accept a couple's claim that they were married. But we know from contemporary sources that this was not at all the case, and that parish authorities would check up on such people. At a time when the welfare system was organised on a local basis, *not* checking the marital status of incomers could mean that the parish became liable for the upkeep of any illegitimate children born to them. In any case, what we now know about the extent of formal marriage in Georgian and Victorian England shows that very few couples lived together without going through a formal ceremony of marriage (see p. 35).

Common mistakes about the law of marriage

Alongside such basic misunderstandings about how the law of marriage works, there are two key mistakes, frequently encountered by genealogists, that have been made about specific aspects of the law.

Mistake No. 1: 'Before the Marriage Act of 1753, all that was needed to create a valid marriage was an informal exchange of consent'

This is the commonest and most entrenched mistake that genealogists will meet when trying to understand how people married in past centuries. Its ubiquity in popular guides to family history means that genealogists risk seriously misinterpreting the evidence their ancestors have left behind. To give readers an illustration, it is worthwhile quoting some examples here.

The most recent print edition (2008) of the *Who Do You Think You Are? Encyclopedia of Genealogy*, for example, is wrong when it says that 'Until 1753, one could marry simply by exchanging vows in public or private without the need of a priest or witnesses. Such marriages were legally recognized'. The *Oxford Companion to Family and Local History* (2010) similarly says that 'marriage by the simple process of affirmation before witnesses was no longer recognized by the law' after 1754, implying that it previously had been. *Ancestral Trails* (2010) has it that an 'exchange of vows by the couple was sufficient under English law', and that 'until Hardwicke's Marriage Act of 1753, a marriage was valid under common law if each spouse had merely expressed (to the other) an unconditional consent to the union.' *Marriage Laws, Rites, Records & Customs* (1996) states that 'a legal marriage anywhere in the British Isles required only mutual consent and agreement ("self-marriage") between a man and a woman…. [A] ceremony, priest or other celebrant, witnesses and festivities were unnecessary.' It would be possible to cite many more examples.

The attentive reader might begin to have doubts, or at least become confused, when reading the conflicting claims about *who* precisely recognised such informal marriages as valid; some guidebooks say that they were not recognized by the Church, but were 'valid under common law'; others claim that it was the Church that recognised a marriage as being created by the exchange of consent alone; some make vague claims about them being accepted as valid marriages by 'the community' and others say that they were frowned upon, but still accepted by the Church *and* the State.

How the mistake came about

So was an exchange of consent regarded as a marriage by either church or state, canon law or common law, or by society in general? The short answer is 'no'. While such claims are mistaken, they are at least excusable. The belief that before 1754 it was possible to marry by a simple exchange of vows is one of long standing, and one that until recently was universally accepted by historians. But it only dates from the nineteenth century, and can be traced to a New York legal case of 1809 and thence to a case heard in England in 1811. The judges in these cases misunderstood the law as it had stood a lifetime earlier, before 1754, and jumped from the fact that a simple exchange of vows had been binding on the parties before this date to the assumption that it must therefore have been a valid marriage for all legal purposes.

The distinction between 'binding' and 'valid'

But being *bound to marry* is not the same as *being married*. The process of getting married before 1754 was rather like buying a house today: a contract binds the parties to go ahead with the sale, but only on completion is title formally transferred and the purchaser permitted to take possession. Similarly, in the context of a marriage, a man and woman did not acquire the legal status of husband and wife until the marriage was formally solemnized before a clergyman.[1]

> **Key fact: before March 25th, 1754, a simple exchange of consent was binding on the parties but not regarded by the law as a marriage.**

Once this point is understood, much that is otherwise baffling about marriage practices before 1754 becomes perfectly explicable. Why, for example, would couples have eloped to remote parishes to be married by an obliging clergyman if they could simply have married by exchanging their vows in private, or before a couple of friends? This argument applies with even more force to the phenomenon of 'Fleet marriages' (see p. 144): the only possible reason for travelling to London's Fleet prison to pay to be married by a clergyman incarcerated there was that his presence was essential to the creation of a marriage.

'Broomstick weddings' and 'hand-fasting'

Once the idea that it was possible to marry by a simple exchange of consent has been shown to be wrong, other claims fall by the wayside—in particular the idea that our ancestors once entered into 'functional' or 'customary' marriages by jumping over broomsticks, by having their hands tied together in 'hand-fasting' rituals or by living together in a 'common-law marriage'.

Again, the roots of these myths have been exposed by recent scholarship.[2] In brief, the idea that it was possible to marry by jumping

---

1 For a detailed analysis of the sources which demonstrate that a simple exchange of vows was not a marriage in and of itself, interested readers are referred to Chapter 2 of *Marriage Law & Practice* (CUP, 2009).
2 Interested readers are referred to Ch.3 of *Marriage Law & Practice* (CUP, 2009).

over a broomstick came about during the nineteenth century because an earlier meaning of the word 'broomstick' had fallen out of circulation. In the 1700s and early 1800s, 'broomstick' was used as an adjective to describe something that was a sham, or was in some way a poor substitute. In drawings from the time, broomsticks appeared as a visual shorthand to make this point, while opponents of civil marriage referred to the act introducing it as the 'Broomstick Marriage Act'. Later generations, unused to this meaning of the word and increasingly open to belief in pre-industrial folk-rituals, mistakenly believed that these were depicting actual ceremonies.

Belief in 'hand-fasting'—often claimed to be a marriage for a year and a day—is also partly rooted in changes in language. It is not uncommon to find references to couples being 'handfast', or to one's 'handfast wife', in early seventeenth-century sources. But this merely denoted a betrothal, a formal contract to marry at some time in the future, and was not any special kind of marriage ceremony. Only much later did it become confused with the (equally mistaken) idea that in Scotland it had been possible to marry for a year and a day.

'Pagan' rites?

Genealogists who have read, or assumed, that these were 'pagan' traditions should ponder the unlikelihood of pre-Christian practices surviving in even the most attenuated of forms from an era more than a millennium earlier, from which there survive only sparse accounts of social practices. It should ring alarm bells when we consider that 'folk customs' or 'pagan' marriage practices are always claimed to have been popular in physically remote, socially isolated regions, amongst people who were outside the mainstream. Stories abound of 'folk practices' in rural Wales or the wilds of the Cumbrian fells, or amongst Gypsies, but they inevitably vanish as we trace them back to their sources. The 'clincher' is that there is not the tiniest scrap of contemporary evidence of any couples ever marrying by jumping a broomstick or by hand-fasting. The only possible conclusion is that such practices never existed. As historians, amateur or otherwise, we should always ensure that the truth *does* stand in the way of what sounds like a good story.

'Common-law marriage': myth and reality

The idea of 'common-law marriage' has an even more convoluted history. In brief, once the nineteenth-century courts had come to the mistaken conclusion that it had been possible to marry by an exchange of consent before 1754, then it also came to be assumed that it would still be possible to marry in this way in those parts of the common-law world where marriage was not governed by statute (see p. 153). This was a convenient assumption at a time when cases were beginning to emerge of marriages celebrated in some far-flung part of the British Empire before a minister who was not a member of the Established Church.

So English law did indeed develop a concept of 'common-law marriage' to deal with marriages of this kind. But not until the 1960s did this become blurred with the American concept of common-law marriage, based on long-term cohabitation, and not until the 1970s did the myth emerge that cohabiting couples in England enjoyed the same rights as married couples as a result of a 'common-law marriage'. The mistaken idea that cohabiting couples in the 1700s and 1800s would have been regarded as having a 'common-law marriage' did not emerge until the 1980s.

Key fact: it was never possible, either before or after 1754, to enter into a 'common-law marriage' in England and Wales.

So, as a serious genealogist you must set aside any possibility that any of your ancestors entered into any kind of 'informal marriage' or 'common-law marriage', or that they jumped a broomstick to marry. It is truly regrettable that the myth of 'common-law marriage' has become so deeply engrained in so short a space of time, since it now genuinely obscures the truth of how our ancestors married before the mid-1700s.

Mistake No 2: 'Any marriage that did not fully comply with Lord Hardwicke's Clandestine Marriage Act of 1753 was void'

Historians have delighted in portraying the 1753 Act as a harsh and draconian measure, and have assumed that every requirement it set out had to be observed in order for the marriage to be valid. This is not excusable, since any attentive reading of the Act's 19 sections (taking up a mere three pages) would quickly dispel such beliefs.

For example, to say that people under the age of 21 had to have parental consent in order to marry, or that the marriage was 'illegal' if it lacked consent, overlooks the fundamental distinction in the 1753 Act between marriages by licence and by banns, and between *active consent* and *lack of dissent* (see p. 113).

Equally misleading, and equally inexcusable, are claims that it was 'compulsory' for marriages to be held in either the bride's or groom's parish. While the 1753 Act did direct that a marriage should take place in the parish where at least one of the parties resided, it also explicitly stated that a marriage could not later be challenged on the basis that this had not been fulfilled (see p. 78).

Finally, it is commonly but mistakenly claimed that the registration of a marriage was essential to its validity. The 1753 Act does not say this, and subsequent case-law established that registration was not a condition of validity (see p. 83).

> **Key fact: while the 1753 Act made certain requirements (i.e. banns or licence, and being married in a church) mandatory, others (the place of marriage, registration, and witnesses) were only directory.**

The reader should be forewarned: in the following pages the emphasis will be on the reality and conformity which formed the background to our ancestors' lives, rather than on dramatic tales of elopements or apparently harsh legal judgments. But if we want to know how our ancestors really lived and loved, we have to look at the past through their eyes, rather than bringing the preconceptions of the twenty-first century to bear. I trust that this book will prove immensely useful and eye-opening.

FURTHER READING

Annal, D. and Collins, A. *Birth, Marriage & Death Records: A Guide for Family Historians* (Pen and Sword, 2012)

Probert, R. *Marriage Law and Practice in the Long Eighteenth Century: A Reassessment* (Cambridge University Press, 2009), ch. 2

Probert, R. *The Legal Regulation of Cohabitation, 1600-2010: From Fornicators to Family* (Cambridge University Press, 2012)

Probert, R. 'Common law marriage: myths and misunderstandings' (2008) 20 *Child and Family Law Quarterly* 1

Probert, R. 'The evolution of the common-law marriage myth' (2011) *Family Law* 283

WHETHER & WHY

HOW MANY COUPLES LIVED TOGETHER
WITHOUT MARRYING?
WHY COUPLES MARRIED
MISTAKEN CLAIMS ABOUT COHABITATION

We should begin by addressing the question of whether, and if so why, your English and Welsh ancestors married. The first is a very basic question for family historians, since one of the most commonly encountered problems of genealogy is that of the untraced marriage: 'I have uncovered an ancestor who had several children by the same woman,' a family historian might observe, 'but for whom I can find no marriage record. They were living at the same address, and I suspect they might have been living together unmarried. Were they *really* married?'

My reply to this would be: 'Yes, they almost certainly went through a formal and legally valid ceremony of marriage, but the record, if it existed, has been lost or destroyed at some point or has simply become untraceable through mis-spelling, mis-filing or mis-transcription.' The reason why this can be stated as a near certainty is that the speculative alternatives that other writers have put forward for 'missing' marriages—'informal' marriage, 'common-law marriage', 'hand fasting' or even marrying by 'jumping the broom'—did not exist in England and Wales (see p. 25). When a couple married, they did so in a way that was formally recognised by the law and which is likely to have been recorded in some form. In addition, detailed local studies have established that all but a tiny fraction of the population married, overturning claims made by some historians about the popularity of cohabitation in earlier centuries.

This is good news for the dedicated family historian, since it increases the likelihood that some record of the marriage exists somewhere, just waiting to be found (and the local studies also point to *where* they may be found, which is discussed further in Chapter Six). Those eager to get on with the task of tracing their ancestors may wish simply to skip ahead to the substantive chapters; but since so many claims about 'alternative' marriage practices have been made, some readers may take more convincing that formal marriage was overwhelmingly the norm for their ancestors. The present chapter provides a distillation of the research that I have undertaken over the last decade and more, which establishes the near-universality of formal marriage among couples who shared a home before the late twentieth century.

How many couples lived together without marrying?

In an age before reliable contraception, a good starting point in answering this question has to be the proportion of births that occurred outside marriage, since most sexual relationships would sooner or later give rise to children. As Fig. 2.1 (p. 32) graphically shows (based on aggregated estimates from hundreds of parishes before 1837, and on the Registrar General's statistics thereafter), the overall proportion of births outside marriage was until recently very low. Nevertheless, when giving talks on the history of marriage I am often amazed by audiences' assumptions that as much as 80 or even 90 per cent of births occurred outside marriage in the eighteenth century! They are frequently surprised to learn that the gallivanting world of Fielding's *Tom Jones* is not an accurate portrayal of eight-eenth-century life.

In fact, at the start of the eighteenth century only around 2% of births occurred outside marriage (the proportion had been even lower during the seventeenth century). This rose gradually over the course of the century, to a little over 5% by 1800. Perhaps surprisingly, it was the mid-Victorian period that saw the highest proportion of births occurring outside marriage, with the rate peaking at just under 7% in the 1860s. It then declined over the second half of the nineteenth century, before rising again in the twentieth. Even then, setting apart

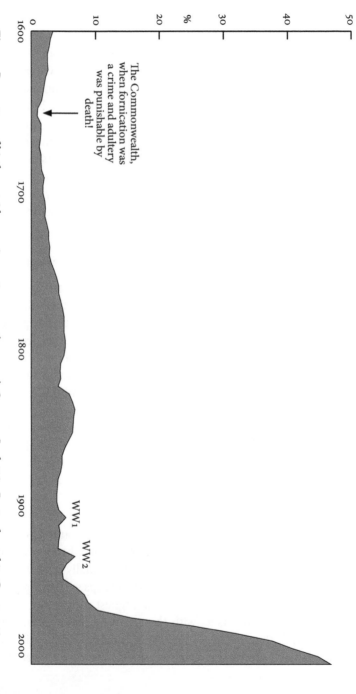

Fig. 2.1 Percentage of births outside marriage, 1600-2010 (see p. 31). Sources: Laslett in *Bastardy and its Comparative History* (Edward Arnold, 1980); ONS; Cambridge Group for the History of Population and Social Structure.

The Commonwealth, when fornication was a crime and adultery was punishable by death!

WW₁

WW₂

those peaks in the proportion (although not the number) of births outside marriage that occurred during the two World Wars, it was only in the 1960s that the illegitimacy rate rose above 6%. By the start of the 1980s it was in excess of 10%, by the end of that decade it was over 30%, and today births outside marriage account for 47% of all births.

But one of my ancestors was definitely illegitimate!

Some people find the evidence of the rarity of illegitimacy in earlier centuries hard to accept. I have had indignant genealogists telling me that they have uncovered an illegitimate ancestor, 'and so has my friend, so that makes two of us, so it can't have been that uncommon!' But it needs to be borne in mind that the likelihood of having an ancestor born outside marriage *at some point* in the last three or four hundred years is far higher than the likelihood of a child being born outside marriage in any given year. My indignant interlocutors also needed to put their illegitimate ancestors in the context of all the legitimate ones that they *had* found.

This is, of course, not to say that people did not have sex with people to whom they were not married (so much is clear from the proportion of babies born not long after a wedding), but for most of our period the vast majority of pre-marital pregnancies resulted in a marriage, whether bargained for or otherwise.

In thinking about why any particular woman did not marry the father of her child, we need to bear two key points in mind: firstly, in an era with relatively high rates of disease and of accidental (or wartime) death, there was always a small but real possibility that a father might die before he had the chance to marry his pregnant sweetheart; secondly, at a time when divorce was rare and expensive, sexual encounters where either or both of the parties was already married to a third person might result in a child which could not be legitimated. Often it will be impossible for family historians to ascertain the truth: was my own grandmother, born in 1917 to an unmarried domestic servant, the result of a romance with a soldier who died fighting for King and country in the trenches, or of a one-off seduction by the head of the household where she was employed?

What we do know is that the minority of conceptions outside marriage that did not result in a wedding usually resulted in the mother bringing up the child alone, or with the support of her parents, rather than sharing a home with the father. Not every paterfamilias rejected his errant daughters, but any examination of workhouse records will always reveal a number of single women and their newly-born children—and no-one went to the workhouse if they had anywhere else to turn. Studies of all Northamptonshire baptisms in the early 1700s, and of baptisms across various counties in the 1800s, suggest that before the twentieth century somewhat under 1% of births can be attributed to mothers who were living unmarried with the father.

But how can we be sure people married?

Sceptical readers might object that if the parents' unmarried relationship was accepted by the community as an 'informal marriage' then the child would not have appeared as 'illegitimate' in the register in the first place, or even that illegitimate children were unlikely to be registered at all. Both objections can be easily tested and shown to be incorrect.

Rates of registration

First, by cross-referencing children listed in nineteenth-century censuses against their entries in the comprehensive digital index of Births, Marriages and Deaths, it can be shown that there was little if any difference in rates of registration between legitimate and illegitimate offspring. While there was probably some under-registration in past centuries (of both legitimate and illegitimate births), it is highly implausible that under-registration could have been so extensive as to account for the great difference between, say, the mid-nineteenth century and the early twenty-first.

Tracing marriages for entire cohorts and communities

Secondly, large-scale studies tracing whether the parents of children named in censuses and parish listings had gone through a ceremony of marriage establish very high levels of marital conformity. Working from baptism registers in the 1700s and census data in the 1800s, covering a range of locations from rural Devon to industrial Salford and from remote Westmorland to urban parishes in York, I have investigated the marital status of over 5,000 couples. In almost all cases it proved possible to trace a record of the marriage. Some, of course, proved easier to find than others (see Figs. on p. 143 and p. 151), while a few proved impossible to verify for reasons that will be familiar to the family historian (common names, suspected mis-recordings, unexplained locations…). Those who were passing themselves off as married without being so at the time of the census (usually ascertained because a later marriage was traced) accounted for a tiny 0.1% of the 5,000 couples examined.

So why have other historians claimed the contrary?

Readers who have been tracing their family tree for some time will appreciate how much easier the basic work has become in recent years. When I was helping my parents back in the 1980s, it was a matter of reading through parish registers, generation after generation, keeping an eye out for a familiar name. Now, of course, the digitization of resources allows potential matches to be identified much more easily.

To show just how much difference this makes, let me give an example. As recently as the 1990s, the historian Barry Reay carried out a similar study to the one described above, for the Kentish parishes of Dunkirk and Hernhill. He looked at couples listed in the 1851 census and tried to trace a marriage for each one. However, because of the arduous nature of searching through parish registers in those days, he only looked at the parish of residence and the parishes where the man, the woman, and their eldest child were born, and managed to trace marriages for only 70% of couples. He therefore assumed that a significant proportion of the rest must have been cohabiting, and later historians have relied on this as evidence of widespread cohabitation.

When I myself used Reay's methodology for a test parish (Kilsby, Northamptonshire, where I grew up), the result was similar—in fact, my success rate was even lower than his, at only 67%. But with modern digital resources, however, it proved possible to trace an entire 100% of marriages, an object lesson in how very unwise it would be to infer that cohabitation had been common from studies using the arduous, old pre-digital methodology.

But were they *validly* married?

One final objection to the argument that marriage was almost universal might be that finding evidence of a marriage is not the same as showing that the couples were *validly* married. This is of course true, and the chapters that follow will show exactly when a marriage might not have been valid. But we should think carefully about what a finding of, say, bigamy, or a marriage within the prohibited degrees actually tells us. Why did the couple feel the need to go through a ceremony in the first place if living together unmarried was as common and acceptable as some have claimed? It was only in the late twentieth century, as unmarried cohabitation became increasingly widespread and socially acceptable, that bigamy became an increasingly infrequent—and unnecessary—crime (see p. 55). Conversely, the much higher incidence of bigamy in previous generations must alert us to the fact that living in a secretly bigamous marriage, albeit illegal and invalid, was more acceptable than the social stigma that came with openly 'living in sin', so vitally important was the status of marriage.

And this observation brings us on to the structural, social and legal reasons that made living in an unmarried sexual relationship quite such an undesirable and rare practice in earlier centuries.

WHY COUPLES MARRIED

Fear of punishment

We must first of all bear in mind that the great majority of the population throughout the seventeenth and eighteenth centuries were church-going, God-fearing Anglicans: the Church taught that fornication was a sin, and that punishment awaited fornicators in the hereafter. Couples who were known to have engaged in sexual relations without going through a valid ceremony of marriage could also be required to do penance in the here-and-now, standing before their church congregation dressed in a white sheet with a suitable look of contrition upon their faces. Even couples who had exchanged vows in words of the present tense (saying to each other 'I take thee for my wife' and 'I take thee for my husband' during, for example, a ceremony of betrothal) could be required to solemnise their vows in church, and could still be punished for fornication if they had sex between the betrothal and the church ceremony. A continued refusal to marry in church could be punished by excommunication. Even the mere suspicion amongst one's neighbours that a couple were living together unmarried could be enough to have them hauled before the diocesan Correction Court to answer the charges. Examples of individuals being punished by the church courts for fornication can be found as late as the 1770s, although by this time it had become extremely rare.

Insurance against destitution

It is often assumed that the poor had little reason to marry, since they had little if any property to pass on to their heirs. One even finds this groundless assumption being perpetuated in university textbooks: *Family Law, Gender & the State* (2012), for example, has it that 'The majority of the population for whom property questions were irrelevant had no need to conform to the rituals of the church'. But if we reflect more deeply for a moment we should realise that poverty would make it all the more important for the poorest to ensure that what scant property they owned *did* pass to their spouse and children, which would certainly not have been the case if they had died intestate and unmarried. At the lowest levels of society, a very little might make the difference between subsistence and destitution.

Of even greater practical importance to the poor, though, and intimately linked to the administration of the church, were the laws on 'settlement'. Before the days of universal social welfare, each and every person in the jurisdiction was by law 'settled' in (that is to say, for certain legal purposes they belonged to) a particular parish. These laws placed financial responsibility for the care of any destitute persons who were legally settled in any given parish squarely upon the shoulders of the other parishioners. Since a wife took her husband's parish of settlement upon marriage, and any legitimate children their father's parish of settlement at their birth, the question of whether or not a couple were validly married was a vital and pertinent question for the parish officers who examined destitutes applying to them for poor relief. Since the upkeep for a destitute illegitimate child would by law generally fall upon the parish in which it was born, it was in the parish's interest to closely ascertain the marital status of its expectant mother before deciding either to allow her to stay or to hurry her along to a different parish.

An unmarried woman, by contrast, retained her own place of settlement, with the result that a couple found not to be validly married could be forcibly returned to their differing parishes of settlement, and their illegitimate children taken from them and returned to the various parishes of their birth, in which they had their own settlement. The laws of settlement, as one might imagine, exercised a powerful influence upon the decision to marry for members of the community: if misfortune did at any time strike, a married couple and their children would at least have the right to poor relief from a single parish rather than face the real and awful prospect of being divided amongst their differing parishes of settlement.

In 1834 the rule was changed so that illegitimate children born after this date would take the settlement of their mother. While this ameliorated one problem, the 'New Poor Law' introduced in that year made it far harder for unmarried mothers to obtain maintenance from the father of their child. In addition, the tendency through the nineteenth century of allotting charity only to the 'deserving' would make it harder for the unmarried mother to win the sympathy of the overseers of the poor. Well into the twentieth century, then, there were good reasons to marry before the birth of a child in order to be as sure as one could be of support.

Ensuring the legitimacy of children

There was another practical reason to marry before the birth of a child. English law resolved in the 1200s that children born outside marriage would be illegitimate, and could not be legitimated by the subsequent marriage of their parents. This remained the case until the twentieth century: not until 1926 did the law allow children to be legitimated by a later marriage, and until 1959 it was a condition of legitimation that the parents had been free to marry at the time of the child's conception or birth. (These legal requirements may also explain some otherwise baffling second ceremonies.) In the eyes of the law, illegitimate children were not even related to their parents or wider kin, and so would not be entitled to inherit anything if their parents died intestate (a rule that did not change until 1969). And if a will left property to the children of those parents, the illegitimate would not be entitled to inherit unless they were explicitly identified by name or implicitly by description (as when, for example, a will referred to 'children' when there was only one legitimate child). Only in 1987 were most of the remaining legal disadvantages of those born outside marriage finally swept away (and to this day they cannot generally succeed to titles of honour).

Daily life

Perhaps the most powerful—if least tangible—reason why couples married was because it simply made daily life so much easier in many small but cumulatively significant ways. For most, marriage was not a 'choice', any more than putting on clothes before one left the house was a 'choice'. It was what one did so as not to cause trouble for oneself or offence to others. A person's marital status had a powerful effect upon their perceived standing and respectability—their 'good name'—within the community. Such varied aspects of daily living as obtaining credit from a shopkeeper, a character reference for an employer, or a roof over one's head were all dependent on one's good name. Even as late as the 1970s, one finds couples stating that they were choosing to marry because it made renting a home so much easier.

THE UNCONVINCING ARGUMENTS FOR WIDESPREAD COHABITATION IN PAST CENTURIES

Finally, having set out the very practical legal and social reasons why couples *would* wish to marry, we should briefly consider the implausibility of the arguments, commonly repeated in genealogical guides, which hold that large swathes of the population lived together outside formal marriage in past centuries.

Claim No 1: 'The unavailability of divorce meant that couples preferred informal unions'

This theory presupposes that earlier generations thought about the risk of their marriages breaking down and made a deliberate decision not to enter into a union that was legally indissoluble. But if anything the reverse is true: the rise of cohabitation in the 1970s can be directly linked to the rise in divorce, as young couples began testing their relationships before embarking on marriages which now had a greater chance than ever before of ending in divorce. There is simply no evidence that fear of marital breakdown encouraged cohabitation in earlier centuries.

Claim No 2: 'Women wished to retain control of their property'

Propertied women *could* retain control of their property on marriage, by means of a legal settlement. For the majority, with only limited assets, marriage was a far better deal than remaining single, since it (generally) provided the woman with support during the man's lifetime and the likelihood of inheriting his assets when he died. Even if the husband deserted the wife, he still had an obligation to support her (enforceable by the parish or through the courts), which was certainly not the case if the pair had merely been cohabiting. This argument also fails to explain why any man would be willing to live unmarried with a woman if the arrangement was to his disadvantage. Marriage might have had a number of disadvantages for women, but it was certainly better than the alternatives.

Claim No 3: 'It was too expensive to marry formally'

Marriage by banns was relatively inexpensive: one late seventeenth-century writer noted that it cost only 1s for the banns to be called and a further 2s 6d for the marriage itself. By the mid-nineteenth century it was not very much more expensive, with the Registrar General estimating the average cost to be around 12s in 1864. Given that most couples married in their mid-to-late twenties, by which time they had generally saved perhaps £50 (accordingly to one estimate for the late eighteenth century), a modest fee for the wedding would have been no real disincentive. It should also be noted that there is some evidence of clergymen, concerned for their poor parishioners' morals, waiving the marriage fee.

Claim No 4: 'In an agrarian society, couples wished to test each other's fertility before embarking on marriage'

There are three major problems with this claim. Most obviously, pregnancy was no guarantee that there would be children to care for one in old age. Life was simply too uncertain, and readers will appreciate, from studying burial records, how often they record the death of newly-borns or young children. Secondly, this theory just doesn't fit with the pattern of pre-marital pregnancy: if couples only decided to marry once the woman was undoubtedly pregnant, one would expect to find far higher levels of pre-marital pregnancy than in fact existed, and also to find post-marital births most commonly occurring around five months after the wedding (assuming three months for the pregnancy to be confirmed and a further month to call the banns or obtain a licence). In fact, there is no such pattern (see further p. 127). Thirdly, having sex before a wedding, or at the very least before an enforceable promise of marriage, exposed a woman to the very real possibility that she would be abandoned, pregnant and unmarried, by her lover. The lot of the single mother left to the mercy of the parish was an unenviable one.

TO SUM UP...

For most of our period, in fact from 1600 right through to the 1970s, we might answer the dual questions of whether, and if so why, people married with an even simpler: 'Yes, for it was easier than not marrying'. For the overwhelming majority of people over those 370 years, the option of sharing one's home in a long-term, sexual relationship with an unrelated member of the opposite sex without going through a formal, legally-recognised ceremony of marriage was almost inconceivable. A few iconoclasts apart, people married because that was simply what one did. It is only in recent decades, as formal marriage has become one option among several, that we feel the need to justify why some of us choose to marry. If you have a *proven* example of a cohabiting couple among your ancestors, you can be sure they were exceptional.

Of course, not everyone married. A detailed examination of any comprehensive census of a given locality will make it clear that a significant proportion of people remained single, living either alone or more likely with wider family members. In an age before reliable contraception and modern medicine, and with censure or punishment awaiting individuals who transgressed society's moral norms, many more people than today simply remained celibate throughout their lives. This was especially true of women, most notably in the years during and after large-scale conflicts which reduced the numbers of available men. But while investigation of one's wider family tree may reveal single brothers and sisters, for obvious reasons they are less likely to be in the direct line that you are investigating.

In summary: yes, the members of your ancestral family tree in all likelihood did marry, while those who did not marry most likely remained single and childless.

FURTHER READING

Probert, R. *Marriage Law and Practice in the Long Eighteenth Century: A Reassessment* (Cambridge University Press, 2009), ch. 3

Probert, R. *The Legal Regulation of Cohabitation, 1600-2010: From Fornicators to Family* (Cambridge University Press, 2012)

Probert, R. 'Recording Births: from the Reformation to the Welfare Reform Act' in *Birth Rites and Rights* (Hart, 2011), pp 171-185

Probert, R. (ed.) *Cohabitation & Non-Marital Births in England & Wales: 1600-2012* (Palgrave Macmillan, 2014)

On the reasons why marriages might not be readily discoverable, see e.g. Ashurst, D. 'St Mary's Church, Worsbrough, South Yorkshire: A Review of the Accuracy of a Parish Register' (1995) 55 *Local Population Studies* 46

3

WHO

MENTAL CAPACITY TO MARRY
BEING FREE TO MARRY
THE PROHIBITED DEGREES
SAME-SEX 'MARRIAGE'
THE LACK OF OTHER LIMITATIONS ON MARRIAGE

Today, the right to marry is regarded as a fundamental human right: most of the prohibitions on whom one can marry have been removed, and the acceptability of cohabitation and the easy availability of divorce means that there is rarely a need for an unhappy or unfaithful spouse to resort to bigamy if a first marriage fails. For previous generations, though, it was all very different: the prohibited degrees extended beyond close blood relationships to include relationships by marriage, and before the twentieth century there were numerous obstacles to obtaining a divorce. When tracing a family tree, a frisson of excitement always surrounds the discovery of evidence that a marriage might have been bigamous, or illicitly entered into within the prohibited degrees. But a knowledge of the often complex rules on whom any individual could marry is vital in order for the family historian to accurately interpret the evidence of censuses and marriage records.

Of course, even today it is still recognized that the state may legitimately regulate not merely how couples marry, but who can marry whom. While the European Convention on Human Rights declares that 'men and women of marriageable age have the right to marry and found a family,' it goes on to add—crucially—'according to the national laws governing the exercise of this right.' The reference to marriageable age indicates the general rule that individuals must reach a certain maturity in order to be eligible to marry. Since this is not so much a matter of *who* as *when*, it is considered in Chapter Five. A more permanent bar to a proposed marriage would be that the individual in question did not have the mental capacity to marry, and this is considered below.

The key concepts to bear in mind when asking the question 'whom could my ancestors marry?' are:

(i) Did they have the necessary *mental capacity* to enter into the contract of matrimony?

(ii) Were the individuals involved *free to marry*?

(iii) Were they specifically able to marry *each other*?

MENTAL CAPACITY TO MARRY

In the eyes of the Church, whose canon law once regulated marriage, if there was no true consent there could be no marriage: if an individual did not have the mental capacity to marry, any marriage they entered into was void from the start. This general rule was supplemented by legislation in 1742 'to prevent the marriage of lunatics.' Lunacy was a specific legal concept, and the act applied to those whom an inquisition had found to be lunatic, or who had been committed to the care and custody of trustees. Any marriage of such a person, the act declared, 'shall be... null and void to all intents and purposes whatsoever.'

Q. *I have discovered that my ancestor, who married in 1780, was committed to an asylum in 1800. Did this mean that his marriage was void from that date?*

A. No. The crucial question was whether he had the mental capacity to marry at the time of the ceremony. If this was the case, then his subsequent mental state would not invalidate the marriage (or even, until 1937, offer any ground for ending the marriage). By contrast, had he been found insane soon after the marriage had taken place, then a court might well have decided that he had been insane at the time of the marriage as well, and held it to be void accordingly.

In all such cases it fell to the person challenging the marriage to show that the individual in question was not mentally capable of giving consent, rather than for that individual to show that he or she had consented. This was no easy matter. As one nineteenth-century judge declared in *Durham v Durham*, marriage was 'a very simple contract, which it does not require a high degree of intelligence to understand'. The presumption, as always, was that an individual did have capacity to marry and that the marriage was accordingly valid.

But assuming that it could be clearly established that one of the parties was incapable of giving consent, the marriage was void and could be challenged even after the death of either spouse. This remained the law until the Nullity of Marriage Act 1971 put all the grounds of nullity on a statutory footing, specifying that future marriages celebrated without consent would be voidable, rather than void. Since a voidable marriage is valid until declared otherwise, and can only be challenged by one of the parties to it, this was a significant change.

> **Key fact: before July 31st, 1971, any marriage entered into by a person who lacked the mental capacity to understand what they were doing was void.**

By way of alternative, more general grounds of 'unsoundness of mind', recurrent epilepsy and suffering from a mental disorder so as to be 'unfitted for marriage' were introduced by legislation in 1937. These, however, only rendered a marriage voidable and so could not be invoked after the death of either party to the marriage.

What of those who were mentally able to consent but who were forced into marriage against their will? Again, the view of the English courts was that this was void as no true consent had been given: the coerced party was, in effect, mentally incompetent on account of the duress to which they had been subjected. Mere reluctance, however, was not sufficient to invalidate a marriage. Many cases that came before the courts—even ones involving specific threats—were held not to meet the high threshold required for an annulment. It would thus be very unwise for the family historian to interpret any evidence of persuasion or coercion—even assuming such evidence could be found—as proof that a marriage was void in the absence of a decree by a court to this effect.

BEING FREE TO MARRY

English law has always required monogamy: being validly married to one person prevents the formation of a valid marriage to another person during the duration of the existing marriage. In other words, being married means that a person is not free to marry anybody else. It is a very common scenario for family historians to trace the marriage of an ancestor to one spouse, and a subsequent marriage to another spouse. There might not be evidence that the first spouse had died in the interim, or there might be evidence that the first spouse did not die until after the second marriage. What are the options that need to be explored in order to determine the validity of the second marriage?

Was there a divorce?

If the first marriage had been ended by divorce, the parties were then free to marry again. From 1600 through to the late twentieth century, divorce was difficult and expensive to obtain, and the majority of the population only ever expected to go through one legally valid marriage ceremony during their lifetime (though remarriage after the death of a spouse was of course not uncommon). While the breakdown of marriages was always recognized by the legal system to some extent, in that a separation 'a mensa et thoro' could be formally granted by the church courts (and its modern equivalent, judicial separation, by the secular courts after 1857), such separations did not give either spouse the right to remarry, as was confirmed by the Star Chamber in *Rye v Fuliambe* (1602). A second marriage after a separation *a mensa et thoro* was therefore void.

Divorce first became available in the 1660s, when the cuckolded John Manners, Lord Roos, obtained a private Act of Parliament permitting him to marry after his separation from his wife. If an ancestor was rich and influential enough to obtain a private act dissolving their marriage, a family historian will have little difficulty in tracing the details in the statute books and parliamentary

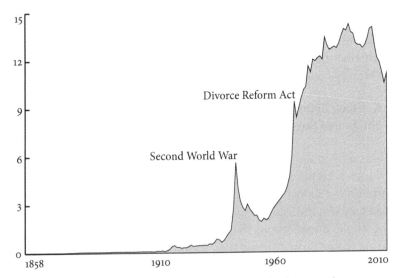

Fig. 3.1 Divorces per 1,000 married couples (see p. 49)

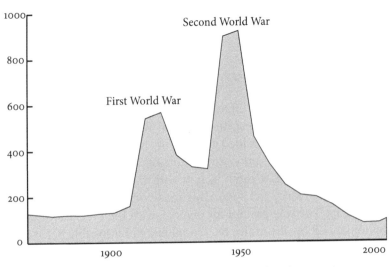

Fig. 3.2 Cases of bigamy known to the police (see p. 56)

debates of the time. (Given that there were only 300 or so individuals who succeeded in obtaining a divorce between the 1660s and 1857, this is a remote scenario for most genealogists!) And if the ancestor whose remarriage is being investigated was a woman, it is even less likely that they obtained a divorce: only four women ever obtained a divorce by means of private Act of Parliament.

Key fact: before 1857, divorce was extremely rare and only obtainable through an Act of Parliament.

It was only under the Divorce and Matrimonial Causes Act 1857 that divorce became more readily available to the general population through the Court of Divorce and Matrimonial Causes in London. Adultery was the sole ground for divorce, and a wife needed to prove not only that her husband had committed adultery but also an aggravating factor (cruelty, desertion, sodomy, bestiality, adulterous rape, or incest). The number of divorces understandably remained low, with only a few hundred being granted each year.

Only in 1923 was the law amended to allow a wife to obtain a divorce on the ground of her husband's adultery alone. After this, the proportion of divorces granted to women rose above 50 per cent, and has rarely fallen below that since.

Key fact: until 1937 divorce was only available on the basis of the other spouse's adultery.

More significant was the effect of the Matrimonial Causes Act 1937, under which the law was again refined to allow a husband or wife to obtain a divorce on the added grounds of cruelty, desertion for three years, or incurable insanity. But the major milestone in the history of English divorce law came in 1971 with the coming into force of the Divorce Reform Act 1969. This made 'irretrievable breakdown of marriage' the sole ground for divorce, with the breakdown being demonstrated by one of five facts: adultery, unreasonable behaviour, desertion for two years, or separation for either two years (if the spouse consented) or five years (if the spouse did not consent).

For the family historian, it is important to note that it was only after January 1st, 1971 that, sooner or later, an unhappy spouse would on one basis or another be able to obtain a divorce and leave behind a marriage they no longer wanted. Fig. 3.1 (p. 47) shows the divorce rate from 1857 to the present day, in order to set the likelihood of a marriage ending in divorce in its contemporary context.

For the rest of the period from 1600 through to the end of 1970, an unknowable number of marriages existed in name only, having broken down in fact but remaining indissoluble in law. The couple who had simply 'grown apart' were unable (short of committing perjury or staging an act of adultery) to divorce and remarry, and any subsequent marriage by either party before the death of their existing spouse was simply void.

Was there an annulment?

But divorce was not the only escape route from a marriage: there was also the possibility of an annulment. This was different from divorce in one crucial respect: annulments were (and still are) granted where there was some impediment to the very existence of the marriage—for example where the parties were too closely related. An annulment is a legal finding that a marriage had never existed. Divorce, by contrast, is a means of ending a valid marriage—or at least this is the meaning of the term today. Considerable confusion has been caused by the fact that an annulment was historically often referred to as a '*divorce a vincula matrimonii*'; Henry VIII, often wrongly assumed to be the progenitor of modern divorce law, actually obtained *annulments* of his marriages to Catherine of Aragon, Anne Boleyn and Anne of Cleves. But annulments, while more readily available than divorce, were still few in number and could only be granted if certain grounds were satisfied. These grounds varied over time, and genealogists investigating an ancestor's marriage need to bear in mind the laws in force at the relevant time.

Factors that have always invalidated a marriage

From 1600 through to the present day, a marriage could (and still can) be annulled if the bride and groom were related to each other within the prohibited degrees (see p. 57); if either was already validly married; if both were of the same sex (before March 13th, 2014) (see

p. 68); if either did not consent to the marriage (see p. 44); or if either was incapable of consummating the marriage. These were all factors existing at the time of the marriage. Even incapacity to consummate, while in many cases only discoverable after the wedding, had to have existed at the time it took place (and be permanent, rather than a temporary incapacity brought about by drinking too much on one's wedding night). This maintained the distinction between annulling a marriage that had never really come into being, and ending an existing marriage by divorce. (Incidentally, sexual satisfaction was not an issue: for a marriage to be consummated it was only necessary for the parties to have had sex once and (to put it delicately) it was not necessary for it to last very long, or for either party to enjoy it!).

Additional factors added over time

In addition to these points, which apart from same-sex marriage have remained unchanged, other factors have at different times affected validity: since 1754 it has been possible to challenge a marriage on the basis that certain formalities, including that of parental consent, have not been observed (although since 1823 it has been necessary to show not just that the couple failed to comply with the law, but that they did so 'knowingly and wilfully': see p. 86); since 1929 it has been possible to challenge a marriage on the basis that one of the parties was under the age of 16 (see p. 110); and since 1937 it has been possible to challenge a marriage on the basis that the bride was pregnant by someone other than her husband-to-be at the time of the marriage, or that one of the parties was suffering from a mental disorder of such a kind as to be unfitted for marriage, was suffering from a venereal disease in a communicable form, or wilfully refused to consummate the marriage (this last being a controversial amendment that blurred the traditional distinction between annulment and divorce, since by definition it occurred after marriage).

'Precontracts'

There was also one ground for annulment, abolished by the 1753 Act, which may be relevant to marriages taking place before that date. This was that one of the parties to the marriage had been 'precontracted' to another person—i.e., there had been an exchange of vows between them such as to create a binding contract to marry that person and no other. But a marriage could not be challenged on the basis of an existing precontract with a third party after the death of either spouse, and indeed it was difficult to challenge a marriage on this basis even while both were alive: two witnesses to the earlier precontract were needed before the courts would annul the later marriage. If such witnesses were forthcoming, and the later marriage was annulled, the parties to the precontract would be obliged to solemnize their marriage in church, the exchange of consent in the precontract not being a marriage in itself (see p. 25). The high standard of proof required meant that it was relatively rare for a marriage to be annulled on the basis of a precontract.

How common were annulments?

Overall, despite this proliferation of grounds, the number of annulments has always been relatively low. Before 1857 it was the task of the church courts to decide whether or not a marriage was valid, and there are no statistics on just how many annulments were granted by local courts. The indications are, however, that the number was not large. Between 1670 and 1857 just under 300 cases of nullity reached the Court of Arches (the appeal court for the entire province of Canterbury) and not all of these resulted in a marriage being declared void. In the same period it has been estimated that the London Consistory Court (the most popular of the lower courts) had just over 200 cases.

After the jurisdiction over marriage passed to the civil courts in 1857, the numbers remained low, with perhaps a couple of dozen cases each year during the remaining decades of the nineteenth century. The number edged upwards during the first decades of the twentieth century, reaching triple figures by the 1930s. It was, however, the Second World War that led to the most dramatic rise: in 1938 there had been 263 petitions for nullity, but by 1947 this figure had leapt to 1,460. In the wake of the war the number of nullity cases subsided, but there were still several hundred each year. The increasing resort to divorce did not mean any reduction in the popularity of nullity as an option: in fact, the number of cases actually increased after the Divorce Reform Act 1969, from 758 in 1968 to 836 in 1973 and 846 in 1986. After this the number fell back, and now runs at a couple of hundred per year.

All this should be borne in mind in assessing the small likelihood that a marriage ended in annulment. And, lest it be thought that the number of annulments granted is a sign of how the law of marriage may trip up unwitting spouses and lead to their marriage being declared void, it should be noted that problems with the solemnization of the marriage have only ever accounted for a tiny number of annulments. By far the most popular ground, from its introduction in 1937 until well into the 1970s, was the other's wilful refusal to consummate the marriage.

Could the first spouse be presumed to have died?

Family history is not short of examples of marital desertion, where one spouse simply disappears one day without a word and never returns. (My own grandfather-in-law, in fact, did just this in the 1940s, leaving a string of abandoned families but only going on to formally remarry in South Africa after the death of his legal wife.) What then could the abandoned spouse do? It would be unjust to leave him or her without any possibility of entering into a new, legally recognised relationship, yet at the same time the law could not simply ignore the fact that the first marriage had never formally been ended. Similar problems arose if one spouse embarked on a foreign journey and was never heard of again.

In the early part of the period, even lengthy absences did not necessarily raise any presumption that the absent spouse had died. By the nineteenth century, however, the advent of railway systems and the telegraph meant that it was far more likely that anyone who was still alive would be able to contact friends and family within a relatively short period of time. It also meant that *not* hearing from someone, and not being able to discover anything of them even after making inquiries, might begin to raise doubts as to whether they were still alive. At around this time the courts developed a presumption that, if a spouse had not been heard of for seven years, by those who could be expected to have heard from them, and inquiries had not discovered their whereabouts, it could be presumed that they had died, leaving the abandoned spouse free to remarry.

Key fact: if a person disappeared and was not heard of for seven years, it could be presumed that they had died.

If the validity of that subsequent marriage were ever challenged in court, then so long as the vanished spouse had not in the meantime turned up the marriage would be upheld as valid. In addition, if there were good evidence that the first spouse had died, then the surviving spouse would be able to marry even before the seven years had elapsed.

Q. *I have found that my ancestor married one man in 1840 and another in 1846 but cannot find any record of the first husband dying. Was the second marriage void and bigamous?*

A. Not necessarily. There was a similar case from this period where the first husband left his wife to travel overseas in 1845. Later that year she received a letter saying that he had died of 'a black fever' at Marseilles. Four years later she married another man. When the validity of that second marriage was later challenged, the court held that the fact that the wife had received information to suggest that the first husband had died, coupled with the fact that he had not turned up in the intervening years, was sufficient to assume that the second marriage was valid.

If, though, the vanished spouse did at any time reappear, the abandoned spouse's subsequent marriage would be void. This was the case even if a court had previously assumed it to be valid. In this not-uncommon scenario, the order of events was crucial:

Q. *I have found a burial record for my ancestor's first wife, but her death occurred after he had married his second wife. Was the second marriage valid from the date of the first wife's death?*

A. No. If a person is not free to marry on the date that the marriage is solemnized, the marriage is void and does not become valid simply because the first spouse later dies.

Q. *My great-grandmother was deserted by her first husband before 1901 and married her second husband in 1908. She then went through a second ceremony of marriage with the second husband in 1920. What might explain this?*

A. The most likely explanation is that she assumed that she was free to marry after seven years had passed, but later discovered that her first husband was still alive. The timing of the second marriage in 1920 might be because there was then conclusive evidence that the first husband was dead or because a further seven years had passed since anyone had heard of him.

Looking at things from the other angle, the 'guilty' spouse who vanished without a word was never in a position to remarry validly, even if for seven years they had not contacted their abandoned spouse: any marriage ceremony the vanished spouse went through would be bigamous (and so a criminal offence), unless he or she had good reason to believe that the first spouse had died in the meantime.

Only after 1937 was it possible for an abandoned spouse to obtain a court decree that would enable them to enter into a second marriage that would not be open to challenge. The Matrimonial Causes Act 1937 introduced the concept of a 'decree of presumption of death and dissolution of marriage'. This did exactly what its title suggested: it presumed that the first spouse was dead and terminated the marriage, leaving the abandoned spouse free to remarry. Even if the vanished spouse later turned up alive and well, the abandoned spouse's second marriage was still valid.

In short, there were many ways in which a second marriage might be valid in the eyes of the law, despite there being no conclusive evidence of the death of the first spouse.

Was the second marriage bigamous?

All this raises a further question: if the abandoned spouse's second marriage was void on account of the vanished spouse still being alive, was the abandoned spouse automatically guilty of bigamy when he or she remarried? The answer is 'not necessarily'. A second marriage under these circumstances could be void without being bigamous. Different areas of law, with different rules and standards of proof, govern whether a marriage is valid as a matter of civil law and whether the criminal offence of bigamy has been committed.

Key fact: a marriage may be void on account of an earlier marriage without being bigamous.

Bigamy was governed by statute as early as 1603, when legislation made it a felony punishable by death. However, it was a defence to show that the other spouse had been absent for seven years (whether overseas or in unknown whereabouts) or that the church courts had granted either a separation *a mensa et thoro* or an annulment of the first marriage. (In the case of a separation the second 'marriage' would still be void, and further legislation in 1828 excluded the defence of an earlier separation.) Even if no defence could be established, the death penalty was rarely exacted, and legislation in 1795 substituted transportation to the colonies. Since those who were transported might enjoy a fair degree of freedom—including, ironically, that of forming new relationships—those whose ancestors were convicted of bigamy may suddenly find that they have a previously undiscovered set of Australian relatives. By the mid-nineteenth century, however, transportation was no longer an option, and the Offences Against the Person Act 1861 substituted a maximum of seven years' imprisonment, which remains the law today.

How common was bigamy?

Those who have found possible evidence of their ancestors entering into multiple marriages may be wondering just how common bigamy actually was. Just as it is unreasonable to take the relatively low number of divorces in 1900 as evidence that there were relatively few broken marriages at that time, so it is unreasonable to project the high divorce rates of our own times back into the past and assume therefore that vast numbers of marriages in previous generations had broken down and persisted in name only. Even today, of course, most marriages do not end in divorce, and in earlier centuries the vast majority would have ended only with the death of one of the parties.

But while we can be reasonably certain that desertion, separation and bigamy were relatively rare events, putting any kind of figure on just how rare is more difficult. Before the mid-nineteenth century we do not even have the assistance of reliable criminal statistics that might show us the number of cases that led to a prosecution for bigamy. Throughout the late seventeenth and eighteenth centuries the Old Bailey (London's central criminal court) heard perhaps two dozen cases each year, but we do not know how representative this one court was. The rise in such cases in the early nineteenth century might have reflected an increase in the extent of bigamy, as urbanisation and improved transport made it easier to travel further and faster and to disappear within the anonymity of the new cities, or it might simply have reflected improved rates of detection and willingness to prosecute.

More reliable bigamy statistics are available from the nineteenth century, and Fig. 3.2 (p. 47) shows the number of cases known to the police from 1880 to the end of the twentieth century (since when the numbers have plummeted still further).

The social disruption caused by the two world wars is evident: bigamy was understandably more common when war gave rise to mass movements of populations and put enormous strain on relationships. Just as interesting, though, is the fact that the inter-war figures never fell back to their pre-war level. The same was true, as Fig. 3.1 showed, of the number of divorces. This would suggest that the relationship between the extent of bigamy and the availability of divorce is not a simple one, and that an increase in the overall rate of marital breakdown may lead to a rise in both divorce and, if that is unavailable or undesirable, bigamy.

The extent of bigamy is, however, a good gauge of the unacceptability of unmarried cohabitation: the fact that cases of bigamy fell in the 1960s was not due to the greater availability of divorce, but the growing acceptability of cohabitation as an alternative, a trend even more marked in the 1970s and 1980s. Finally, it should be noted that bigamy has tended to be a male crime, with female bigamists accounting for a little over 20% of the total throughout the period for which statistics are available.

Readers who have already discovered a bigamous ancestor, or who suspect that they might have, are directed to my 2015 book *Divorced, Bigamist, Bereaved?*, which covers the subject of bigamy in much greater detail.

THE PROHIBITED DEGREES

Throughout the period from 1600 to the present day, individuals have been restricted as to whom precisely they might marry by legal prohibitions on marriage within defined degrees of consanguinity (i.e. between blood relations) and affinity (i.e. between in-laws). The exact details of these prohibitions are complicated, and have changed across the centuries (in fact, they were last updated as recently as 2007). Marriages between certain persons have always been valid, while the legal status of others has varied, as set out below.

But while the prohibited degrees are complex, and the consequences of entering into a prohibited marriage have not been static, the genealogist can at least be reasonably certain of the facts. Unlike other circumstances that might render a marriage void—a failure to comply with specified formalities, for example—the fact that two people are related within the prohibited degrees is something that can be ascertained with a fair degree of certainty. And while the precise degrees within which marriage was prohibited could and did vary over time, whether any two people were within the prohibited degrees at any given time depended only on the law and not on changes in the family relationship. To put it another way, a man remained related to his wife's sister even after the death of his wife: indeed, this was the relationship that generated more discussion and controversy than any other, as we shall see.

The possibility of petitioning Parliament to pass a private Act allowing a particular marriage to go ahead (as in, for example, the Edward Berry and Doris Eileen Ward (Marriage Enabling) Act 1980, which permitted a marriage between a former step-father and step-daughter) is one that need not trouble the family historian too much. Few such Acts were ever passed, certainly far fewer than the 300 or so Acts permitting divorce.

For ease of reference, the prohibited degrees are set out in Table 3.1 (overleaf) in as simple a way as possible, in order to alert the reader to those relationships that might be problematic and to those that would not have been subject to any challenge.

Never valid	Varied over time (see Tables 3.2 and 3.3)	Always valid
parent/child	spouse's parent/child	cousins
grandparent/ grandchild	parent's/child's spouse	adoptive relations other than parent/ child
sibling	spouse's grandparent/ grandchild	
aunt/uncle	grandparent's/grand- child's spouse	
niece/nephew*	spouse's sibling	
	sibling's spouse	
	spouse's aunt/uncle	
	spouse of aunt/uncle	
*except 1650-60 (see below, p. 60)	spouse's niece/nephew	
	spouse of niece/nephew	

Table 3.1 (see p. 57)

In order to understand precisely which relations it was possible to marry at any given time, and what the consequences of such a marriage would be, we need to look at how the law developed and changed.

The position in 1600

Those who have whiled away lengthy sermons by peeking at the list of persons with whom marriage is forbidden in the *Book of Common Prayer* will already be familiar with Archbishop Parker's table of prohibited degrees. First drawn up in 1563, it was explicitly stated in 1604 that marriages within the specified degrees would be 'adjudged incestuous and unlawful' (Canon 99). Public familiarity with the prohibitions was increased by the requirement that churches should display Parker's table in some prominent place. This table, while lengthy, was considerably shorter than in earlier centuries. Prior to the English Reformation in the sixteenth century, the prohibited degrees had been very extensive, but their rigour was mitigated by the possibility of obtaining a dispensation from the Pope to allow a particular couple to marry. Come the Reformation, legislation was passed to create absolute prohibitions on marriage within a narrower range of relatives. The list of relatives whom one was prohibited from marrying included, as one would expect, close blood relations. So an individual was prohibited from marrying a parent or child, who were regarded as being within the 'first degree of consanguinity', or a grandparent, grandchild or sibling (full or half), who fell within the 'second degree'. Marriages with uncles and aunts, or nieces and nephews, who were regarded as being within the 'third degree', were also prohibited. There were, however, no prohibitions on marriages between cousins or more remote kin.

Key fact: marriages between cousins have never been invalid under English law.

Less intuitively to modern sensibilities, from before the Reformation until well into the twentieth century the prohibited degrees also included relations by marriage. In the eyes of the Church, and therefore of the law, husband and wife became 'one flesh' on marriage, so the wife's relatives became the husband's (and vice versa) and remained so even after the death of one of the parties to the marriage. As a result, one could also not marry a former spouse's parent, child, grandparent, grandchild, sibling (full or half), uncle, aunt, niece or nephew. However, one spouse's relatives were not regarded as themselves being linked to the other spouse's relatives, so that a marriage between a woman's sister and her husband's brother was perfectly valid (and not uncommon).

It should be noted that the prohibitions as set out in Parker's table were more logical than their original Biblical inspiration. The Book of Leviticus set out a number of relationships that should not have a sexual dimension (or in the words of the original, 'None of you shall approach to any that is near of kin to him, to uncover their nakedness'). Included in this list was the wife of one's son or brother. By parity of reasoning, a relationship between the sister of one's wife was deemed to be the same as one with the wife of one's brother. However, Leviticus 18:18 said something slightly different, merely instructing a man not to marry his wife's sister during the wife's life time, while the Book of Genesis, in the story of Jacob, Leah and Rachel, actually provided a precedent for marrying two sisters. Small wonder, then, that the prohibition on a marriage between a man and his deceased wife's sister was to attract more controversy, and more challenges, than all the rest put together. As a result, the family historian is more likely to find such unions than any others within the prohibited degrees.

One further controversy was whether sexual intercourse, as well as marriage, brought the kin of the two individuals within the prohibited degrees. This was the justification relied on by Henry VIII when dissolving his marriage with Anne Boleyn, as he had previously had a sexual relationship with her sister. Of course, the fact that Anne was subsequently executed removed any obstacle to Henry's next marriage. The genealogist despairing of uncovering evidence of sexual relationships which would have proved to be a bar to a marriage should be reassured by the fact that when a court was eventually called upon to determine this point in the mid-nineteenth century it was decided that no such prohibition existed. It was also pointed out that there had been no cases of marriages being annulled on this basis in the previous 300 years, so this at least is one avenue that need not be explored by the family historian!

Under the Commonwealth

Legislation passed in 1650 narrowed the range of relations with whom marriage was forbidden, but increased the penalties for those who did enter into such a marriage. From June 24th, 1650, a marriage between a person and the following kin was void: parent or child; grandparent or grandchild; sibling; aunt or uncle; parent's or child's spouse; spouse's parent or child. More dramatically, the penalty for any sexual relationship between those so nearly related was to 'suffer death as in case of Felony'.

From the Restoration to 1835

At the Restoration in 1660 the old rules were restored, and as a reminder were set out in the 1662 *Book of Common Prayer*. But the reduced power of the church courts led to a change in the *consequences* of marrying. From the late seventeenth century, a marriage within the prohibited degrees could not be challenged after the death of either party. This was due to the intervention of the common-law courts, which were constantly battling with the church courts for supremacy. In practical terms, a common-law court could issue an order preventing the church courts from hearing a dispute over the validity of a marriage after the death of one of the parties. In legal parlance, a marriage within the prohibited degrees between 1660 and 1835 was therefore *voidable* rather than void.

Key fact: a marriage within the prohibited degrees could only be challenged while both parties to it were alive.

It is important to understand what was meant by 'voidable' at the time, since there is an important difference between the way the term is used now and the way it was used then. Today, only the parties to a voidable marriage have the ability to challenge it, but this was not the case in earlier centuries. Even if the marriage was happy, and neither party wished to challenge its validity, there was always the risk that some third party might bring an action and obtain an annulment on the grounds that the parties were within the prohibited degrees. In one case from 1811 it was the husband's sisters who brought the suit to annul his marriage to his late wife's sister, clearly motivated by the fact that they stood to inherit under their mother's will if their brother died without lawful issue. Five years later, the court heard another case where it was the churchwardens, who disapproved of what they thought an 'incestuous' marriage, who instigated the legal challenge.

For the genealogist, the most important point to take from these rather complicated legal arguments is that a marriage within the prohibited degrees which was not challenged and annulled during the lifetime of the parties was valid in the eyes of the law, and any children were accordingly legitimate.

In theory, this was the case however closely the couple were related. The point remains at the level of legal theory because the cases that came before the courts invariably involved individuals who were related by marriage rather than by blood. One should bear in mind the unlikelihood of a marriage taking place between, say, a father and his daughter or between brother and sister. More likely, though, would be the unintentional marriage of two half-siblings, or perhaps a woman and her nephew If the parties had been unaware of their consanguinity before their marriage, and only later discovered it, the chances were that they would regard their union as immoral and unlawful and agree to separate. If they never discovered the truth of their consanguinity during their own lifetimes, it is unlikely that anyone else would do so, either before or after their deaths. The rare genealogist who uncovers evidence of a consanguineous marriage should assume, if no evidence comes to light that the marriage was annulled within the parties' lifetimes, that it was nevertheless valid.

Key fact: a marriage that was never challenged should be regarded as having been valid.

Whether or not the marriage *was* annulled will not be easy to ascertain: by no means every case was reported, and the copious records of the church courts have only rarely been transcribed. Many cases, however, will have been indexed, and the time-frame within which it is necessary to search will be limited to the joint lives of the parties. If you have traced a marriage within the prohibited degrees, it would be worthwhile exploring the other resources of the county record office to see if the validity of the union was ever challenged.

Of course, as with a number of other requirements of marriage law, the pragmatic aim was to prevent, rather than undo, marriage within the prohibited degrees. Most people would never even have contemplated such a marriage; the cases that tended to occur were ones where there was some genuine ambiguity about the legality and morality of the union, such as that between a man and the sister of his deceased wife. In such cases, the challenge was finding a clergyman to conduct the marriage in the first place. If the local clergyman were approached to celebrate a marriage between a man and the sister of his deceased wife, he would be likely to refuse. But if the pair could marry where they were not known then there would be no obvious reason for a clergyman not to conduct the ceremony. The inventor Matthew Boulton adopted this route, secretly marrying his deceased wife's sister in London in 1760. In the absence of any subsequent challenge, the pair lived happily ever after, validly married.

Another area of ambiguity was the position of illegitimate children. An illegitimate was, in the eyes of the law, 'nobody's child'. As a matter of logic, then, such children were not related to their parents and thus not within the prohibited degrees in relation to them.

Q. *I have discovered that my ancestor was born out of wedlock in 1780. Her mother later married a different man, but died in child-birth. My ancestor then married her mother's widower! Was this legal? If not, why did the vicar allow the ceremony to go ahead?*

A. There was enough uncertainty as to their legal position to allow such a marriage to go ahead. A marriage between a man and his deceased wife's daughter was within the prohibited degrees (and remains subject to certain restrictions to this day). But since an illegitimate child was *filius nullius*, 'nobody's child', it followed that the prohibited degrees could not apply. As late as the mid-nineteenth century this point was still being debated; not until 1861 was it formally resolved that the prohibited degrees applied equally to those born outside marriage. As the court noted, it would be 'a great scandal' if they did not apply, since otherwise 'an illegitimate brother might marry a sister.' But before that date there would have been enough ambiguity for a parson to decide that the marriage could go ahead. In this he might be swayed by the alternatives: if the couple were already living together he might well decide, as one contemporary noted, 'certainly marriage of any kind is some sanction rather than to live together as they did without any sanction in a Moral Sense.'[1]

From 1835 to 1907

In 1835, however, there was a sudden and stark change of policy. Legislation passed in that year provided that, for the avoidance of doubt, all future marriages within the prohibited degrees were to be void rather than voidable, whether the couple were related by blood or by marriage. The need for certainty also prevented the church courts from annulling any marriages that had already taken place within the

1 J. Ayres, *Paupers and Pig Killers: The Diary of William Holland, A Somerset Parson, 1799-1818* (Sutton, 2003), p. 190.

prohibited degrees of affinity (i.e. between in-laws), unless they had already been challenged and declared null, or where a challenge to the marriage was before the courts. This meant that such marriages entered into before 1835 were effectively rendered valid. Marriages before 1835 within the prohibited degrees of consanguinity (i.e. between blood relations) remained voidable:

	Celebrated before August 31st, 1835	Celebrated after August 31st, 1835
Parent/child	Voidable	Void
Grandparent/ grandchild		
Sibling		
Aunt/uncle		
Niece/nephew		
Spouse's parent/child	Valid	
Parent's/child's spouse		
Spouse's grandparent/ grandchild		
Grandparent's/grand- child's spouse		
Spouse's sibling		
Sibling's spouse		
Spouse's aunt/uncle		
Spouse of aunt/uncle		
Spouse's niece/nephew		
Spouse of niece/ nephew		

Table 3.2 Status of marriages within the prohibited degrees after August 31st, 1835 (see p. 63)

As noted above, in 1861 it was confirmed that the prohibited degrees applied to those born outside marriage. But other questions remained:

Q. *I have discovered that in 1850 my great-great-grandfather travelled overseas to get married in a country that permitted marriages between in-laws, as he was marrying the sister of his deceased wife. Would this marriage have been regarded as valid when they came back to England?*

A. No. It was not possible to escape the prohibition on marrying within the prohibited degrees by going overseas. If an individual travelled overseas in order to marry, they had to comply with the formalities required by the country where the marriage was taking place, but their capacity to marry remained governed by English law, which forbade a man from marrying the sister of his late wife.

Q. *I have discovered that my great-great-grandfather was living with a woman outside marriage, and then ran off with her sister! Was their subsequent marriage valid?*

A. Yes. If he had married the woman with whom he had been living, then there would have been a legal bar to his marrying her sister, even after his wife's death (and even more obviously before!). But merely living (and presumably having sex) with a woman did not create any relationship of affinity with her kin.

Q. *I've read that Jewish law permitted a man to marry his niece, or his deceased brother's widow. Were such marriages valid in England?*

A. Not if the parties were resident in England at the time of the marriage. Litigation in 1900 established that the privilege enjoyed by the Jews as to marrying according to their own usages (see p. 103) only applied to the *form* of the marriage. Their *capacity* to marry was governed by English law, and this remained the case even if they travelled overseas in order to marry. However, if an uncle and niece were resident in a country that did permit such marriages, married there, and then came to England, the marriage would be recognised as valid.

From 1907 to the present day

By the start of the twentieth century, Biblical teachings were regarded as a less weighty justification for legal prohibitions. There was no wholesale and immediate rejection of the principle that marriage created links that should act as a bar to a subsequent marriage; instead, practical considerations led to piecemeal reform.

The first prohibition to be removed was that on a marriage between a man and his deceased wife's sister. As noted above, this was the one prohibition for which Biblical authority seemed shaky. It was also the one that there had been the most attempts to remove. In practical terms, it was strongly argued that a sister-in-law was the person best placed to care for the bereaved family, and that the bar on marriage was simply creating a class of unmarried unions. In 1907, reform was finally achieved when the Deceased Wife's Sister's Marriage Act was passed, allowing a man to validly marry his deceased wife's sister with no question of voidability or legal challenge, and removing the possibility of future challenge to any such marriages that had already taken place. If the marriage had already been annulled, however, it would remain so.

Key fact: after August 28th, 1907, a marriage between a man and the sister of his late wife was valid, whether it had taken place before or after that date.

Even so, it was to be another fourteen years until any further prohibitions were removed. The Deceased Brother's Widows Marriage Act 1921 was passed in the wake of the First World War, as a response to the plight of those whose husbands had been killed in the war and who had subsequently fallen in love with their former brother-in-law. After July 28th, 1921, such marriages, whether celebrated before or after that date, were valid.

In 1926, however, one new prohibition was *added* to the list. This was as a consequence of adoption being put on a legal footing for the first time. Before this date such adoptions as had taken place had been informal and had not affected the question of legal parenthood. The legislation passed in 1926 created the fiction that an adopted child ceased to be the child of the birth parents and became the child of the adoptive parents. The logic of this, however, was not pushed too far. The adopted child remained within the prohibited degrees vis-à-vis the original birth family. So if a child who had been adopted later inadvertently married a blood sibling, the marriage was void. By contrast, the adoption of a child only created prohibitions on marriage between an adopting parent and their adopted child, rather than with wider adoptive kin. A marriage between an adopted person and their adoptive sibling was perfectly valid, and this remains the case today.

But the general legal trend was towards the removal of prohibitions on marriage. In 1931 further legislation removed the bar on marrying a deceased's spouse's aunt/uncle or niece/nephew. Over the course of the twentieth century, as divorce became more common, the question also arose as to whether it should be possible to marry a former in-law. Not until 1960, however, was legislation passed permitting marriages to take place between a divorcee and their ex-spouse's sibling, aunt/uncle, or niece/nephew (or between an individual and the divorced spouse of their sibling, aunt/uncle, or niece/nephew).

By the 1980s the only relationships by affinity that were still prohibited were those between a parent and the spouse of his or her child, and between step-parent and step-child. A review of the law led to legislation allowing such relationships on certain conditions. Since these are unlikely to be of relevance to current genealogists, the details are not provided here (but the interested can find them in any modern family law textbook). For the sake of completeness, it can simply be noted that restrictions on marriages between step-parent and step-child remain, but those between parent-in-law and son/daughter-in-law were removed in 2007, exactly 100 years after marriage with a deceased wife's sister became lawful.

Relationship	When permitted
Deceased wife's sister	1907
Deceased husband's brother	1921
Deceased spouse's aunt/uncle/niece/nephew	1931
Divorced spouse's sibling, aunt or uncle, niece or nephew	1960

Divorced spouse of sibling,
aunt or uncle, niece or nephew   1960

Former step-child   1986*

Former son/daughter-in-law   2007

(*but only if the relationship had not been that of parent/child)

Same-sex 'marriage'

Before the Marriage (Same Sex Couples) Act 2013, marriage in England and Wales was exclusively heterosexual. Cases did, however, on very rare occasions come before the English courts where a 'married' couple in fact turned out to consist of two people of the same sex. If as a family historian you are lucky enough to uncover evidence or rumour of such a 'marriage', you can be quite certain that it was simply void (rather than voidable) from the start.

The lack of other limitations on marriage

These restrictions aside, anyone is free to marry any other person. Unlike other countries, the law of England and Wales has never based any restrictions on marriage upon the parties' social class or religious faith. Though courts throughout the period might well have bent over backwards to find a way to invalidate an 'unsuitable' match between, say, a scullery maid and an impressionable young aristocrat, there has never been any formal bar to such socially unequal unions. Similarly, English law has never prevented the formation of a valid marriage between, say, an Anglican and a Roman Catholic: so long as the ceremony followed the requirements in force at the time, the parties' faith was and remains immaterial, and religiously mixed marriages were not uncommon.

Key fact: English law has never prevented people of different faiths from entering into a valid marriage together.

Q. *I have discovered that an early nineteenth-century ancestor married a man recorded as being Jewish. Having read that the law forbade the marriage of Jews and non-Jews, I'd like to know whether their marriage was valid or not.*

A. English law has never forbidden the intermarriage of Jews and non-Jews. Some books on family history repeat the mistaken belief that such unions were invalid, and the confusion might have arisen because of the exemption of Jews (and also Quakers) from the requirements of the Marriage Act 1753. Jews and Quakers did not need to marry in church, but the exemption only applied where *both* parties were Jewish or Quaker. From 1754 to 1836, if a Jew married a Gentile the marriage had to take place in the Church of England to be valid. This was tested in the case in *Jones v Robinson* (1815), where a Jewish woman had married a Christian man in a church. Since she was underage and had married by licence without consent, the marriage was void, but there was no suggestion that the pair were otherwise ineligible to marry. If they had married in a Jewish wedding, it would not have been valid since the husband was not Jewish. After 1836 the same restriction continued to apply, but by then mixed-faith couples had the added option of marrying in a civil ceremony.

FURTHER READING

Probert, R. *Divorced, Bigamist, Bereaved?* (Takeaway, 2015)

On mental capacity
Jackson, J. *The Formation and Annulment of Marriage* (Sweet & Maxwell, 2nd ed., 1969)

On divorce
Bailey, J. *Unquiet Lives: Marriage and Marriage Breakdown in England, 1660-1800* (Cambridge University Press, 2003)

Cretney, S. *Family Law in the Twentieth Century: A History* (Oxford University Press, 2003), Part II

Probert, R. 'The Roos Case and Modern Family Law' in *Landmarks in Family Law* (Hart, 2011)

Savage, G. 'The Operation of the 1857 Divorce Act, 1860-1920' (1982) 16 *Journal of Social History* 103

Wolfram, S. 'Divorce in England 1700-1857' (1985) 5 *Oxford Journal of Legal Studies* 155

On annulments
Cretney, S. *Family Law in the Twentieth Century: A History* (Oxford University Press, 2003), ch. 2

On the presumption of death
Stone, D. 'The Presumption of Death: a Redundant Concept?' (1981) 44 *Modern Law Review* 516

On bigamy
Capp, B. 'Bigamous Marriage in Early Modern England' (2009) *The Historical Journal* 537

Frost, G. 'Bigamy and Cohabitation in Victorian England' (1997) 22 *Journal of Family History* 286

On the history of the prohibited degrees
Wolfram, S. *In-Laws and Outlaws: Kinship and Marriage in England* (Taylor & Francis, 1987)

Cretney, S. *Family Law in the Twentieth Century: A History* (Oxford University Press, 2003)

Masson, Bailey-Harris and Probert, *Cretney's Principles of Family Law* (Sweet & Maxwell, 8th ed., 2008), ch 2

❦ 4 ❦

How

Understanding how one's ancestors married is crucial for the family historian: without knowing which options were available, and which popular, it is difficult to know where to look for evidence and impossible to interpret correctly what has been found within the context of those ancestors' lives. This chapter will answer two distinct but related questions: how *could* people marry? (that is to say, what was necessary for a legally binding ceremony), and how *did* people marry? (what forms did their marriages take). This distinction does not imply that significant numbers of people married in ceremonies that had no legal validity; on the contrary, the evidence shows that throughout the period couples complied with what the law required. But it does mean that the family historian needs to know the relative popularity of different options when the law provided more than one legally valid route to matrimony, and how people coped when the legal options were more limited.

Precisely how our ancestors chose to marry is intimately tied up with the history of religion in England and Wales and the popularity of different denominations at different times. The relative strength of the Anglican Church in relation to other faiths and denominations can be illustrated by the fact that the number of nonconformist baptisms remained very low in proportion to Anglican ones—less than 1% before the mid-eighteenth century, and only passing 4% at the start of the nineteenth. Anglicanism's near monopoly on sacramental rites should be borne in mind in assessing the likelihood of one's ancestors even contemplating marrying outside the Church.

This chapter will begin by giving a brief overview of the ways in which it was possible to marry at different times. It will then go on to look in detail at different types of marriage, and how their legal status, consequences, and general popularity changed over time.

A BRIEF TIMELINE AND OVERVIEW

1600-1653 Marriage governed by Anglican canon law

1653-1657 Civil marriage only method permitted: all others void

1657-1660 Civil marriage only method specified, but no provision invalidating other kinds of marriage

1660-1754 Marriage governed by Anglican canon law

1754-1837 Marriage governed by statute: Anglican marriage only method permitted, with limited and uncertain exceptions for Jews and Quakers

1837 to now Civil marriage and marriage according to the rites of other religious denominations permitted as well as Anglican marriage

All this is relatively well known and straightforward, but what the Anglican Church's canon law actually required for a valid marriage has frequently been misunderstood. The fact that the majority of its instructions as to how couples should marry were merely *directory*, and therefore did not affect the validity of the marriage, has led to a mistaken belief amongst some historians that no formalities whatsoever had to be observed. But, as noted in Chapter One, there was one indispensable requirement—the presence of an Anglican clergyman.

The absolute legal necessity for an Anglican clergyman might come as a surprise to genealogists who have read elsewhere that before 1754 it was possible to marry by a simple exchange of vows—that is to say, by each party simply saying 'I do'. Based on this mistaken belief, it has been widely assumed that prior to 1754 it was possible to marry

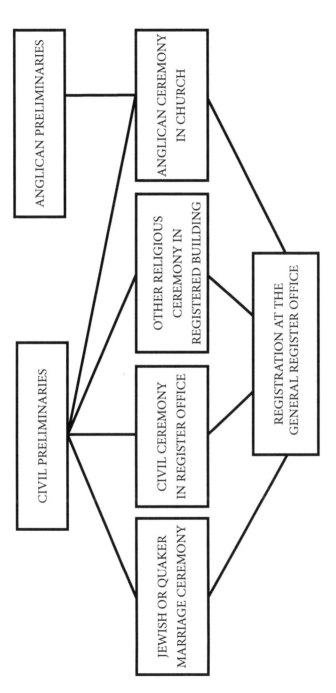

Fig. 4.1 The possible procedures for entering into and registering a marriage under the Marriage Act 1836

The boxes in the figure read:

ANGLICAN PRELIMINARIES

CIVIL PRELIMINARIES

ANGLICAN CEREMONY IN CHURCH

OTHER RELIGIOUS CEREMONY IN REGISTERED BUILDING

CIVIL CEREMONY IN REGISTER OFFICE

JEWISH OR QUAKER MARRIAGE CEREMONY

REGISTRATION AT THE GENERAL REGISTER OFFICE

according to the rites of any religion. The case-law from the time, however, flatly contradicts this: if an exchange of consent was carried out in a *non-Anglican* chapel or before a *dissenting* minister or any other person, it did not create a valid marriage.[1]

The implications for genealogy are profound: if it had been possible to marry by a simple exchange of 'I do', then there would be no record for the family historian to find. But if marriage *had* to be celebrated before an Anglican clergyman and was usually celebrated in church, then the chances are that some record will have been made. Whether the record has survived, and where the marriage actually took place, is another matter, but it is worth continuing to look.

The realisation that an exchange of consent did not create a marriage also affects how family historians must interpret what they have found. Those who have found their ancestors marrying in the Church of England may have assumed that they were unusual, or exceptionally conscientious Anglicans. They were, in actual fact, perfectly unexceptional. Before 1837, when the law changed, there is relatively little likelihood of finding any evidence of marriages being celebrated other than according to Anglican rites.

Key fact: before 1837, couples marrying in England and Wales almost invariably married before an Anglican clergyman, in an Anglican parish church.

It should also be noted that very few would even have wanted to marry outside the Anglican Church: while Catholics, Jews and Quakers did have their own marriage practices even before this date, added

---

1 Some confusion has been generated by the different roles of the church courts and the common law courts. The church courts had exclusive jurisdiction over the question of whether or not a marriage was valid. But the question of whether a particular couple were married might also come before the common law courts, for example, if a husband was sued for debts contracted by his wife. Rather than referring the issue to be determined by the church courts every time it arose, the common law courts simply looked at whether there was evidence that the parties had come through some kind of ceremony and did not enter into the question of whether that ceremony was capable of creating a valid marriage. The details of this complex area are explained in Ch. 4 of *Marriage Law & Practice*.

together such groups were only a tiny section of the population, probably less than two per cent by the mid-eighteenth century.

By the early nineteenth century, however, it was clear that reform was needed. An increase in religious dissent, and changing attitudes toward it, led to calls for other non-Anglican marriages (beside those of Jews and Quakers, whose rather anomalous status is considered below) to be permitted. It was also recognised that there was a need for a new and more centralised system of civil registration to meet the needs of a modern nation. As a result, under the Marriage Act 1836 a whole range of different routes to a binding marriage was introduced. Even so, it was not until the late twentieth century that the majority of marriages took place outside the Anglican Church, and so it is best we begin with the Church's requirements for a valid marriage.

ANGLICAN MARRIAGES

The broad structure of Anglican marriage has changed little since the start of our period and indeed earlier: the calling of the banns was first established as a preliminary in the twelfth century, and the possibility of obtaining a licence to dispense with the banns in 1533. But the devil is always in the detail, and the consequences of failing to comply with the law's requirements have varied at different times.

1600-1653

The Church's 1604 canons reiterated that a marriage had to be preceded by either calling the banns or obtaining a licence. It also required that parental consent be obtained to the marriage of a minor (see p. 111), and that the marriage take place in the church of the parish where at least one of the parties was resident (see p. 136). However, a marriage was still valid if it was celebrated without banns or licence, or even outside the Church (for example in a private house), as long as it was presided over by an Anglican clergyman. Such marriages were termed 'clandestine'.

Key fact: a marriage was regarded as 'clandestine' if it failed to comply with one or more of the requirements of the canon law. Yet as long as an Anglican clergyman had presided, it was nevertheless still valid.

From the Commonwealth to the Restoration

The turbulent years of the Civil War in the 1640s initially made no difference to how people could marry. The Puritan *Directory of Public Worship*, published in 1645, declared that marriage was 'no Sacrament' but grudgingly judged it to be 'expedient' that it be solemnized by a recognised clergyman.

Between 1653 and 1660, however, civil marriage was briefly introduced (see p. 89). What then was the status of an Anglican marriage celebrated during this period if not accompanied by a legally valid civil marriage? Between 1653 and 1657 the law stated that any ceremony other than the civil rite was void, but from June 26th, 1657 this clause was removed, leaving the status of other ceremonies unclear. But the reinstatement of the canon law in 1660 meant that any subsequent challenge to their validity would be unlikely to succeed (even if a marriage had been declared void prior to the Restoration in 1660, later courts could overturn this decision). One case decided in 1661 considered the validity of the dissolution of a marriage celebrated by a clergyman during the Commonwealth era: it was declared that the laws in force during that period were contrary to the law of God, and that the fact that the marriage had taken place before a clergyman did not render it void, no matter what the law of the land had stated at the time.

> **Key fact: although civil marriage was the only stipulated way of entering into a marriage between 1653 and 1660, Anglican marriages were later upheld.**

The family historian who has traced an Anglican marriage for an ancestor during the Commonwealth, but has not found a civil marriage, can be reassured that the marriage would have been regarded as valid within a very short period of time, even if not at the moment of celebration.

From the Restoration to March 24th, 1754

At the Restoration in 1660 the canon law was reinstated, and the old rules restored. The religious turmoil of the preceding years had led to a much clearer definition of what it meant to be an Anglican clergyman, with the Act of Uniformity 1662 stipulating that a clergyman had to be correctly ordained. As a consequence, there was a much sharper delineation of exactly who had authority to celebrate marriages. Restoration-era plays are full of marriages whose validity is questioned on the basis that the person celebrating the marriage was not eligible to do so, and this was clearly a topical issue that would have resonated with audiences. When disputed marriages came before the courts, it was confirmed that the crucial issue was whether or not the man celebrating the marriage was in holy orders, rather than whether the bride and groom believed this to be the case.

Key fact: before March 25th, 1754, neither the Church nor the secular courts regarded as valid any marriage which had not been celebrated before an ordained Anglican clergyman.

For the family historian, the point to bear in mind is that while a marriage could have been challenged at the time on the basis that it had not been celebrated by an ordained clergyman, those that were not challenged then can now be presumed to be valid.

But the restored Church faced other problems. It was not easy re-imposing discipline after the turbulent years of the Common-wealth. The fact that the presence of a clergyman was all that was necessary to create a valid marriage (assuming of course, that the parties were free to marry each other: see Chapter Three) led not just to couples ignoring the stipulations of the canon law and marrying in churches away from their home parish, but also to an increasing number of marriages taking place outside *any* church (see further Chapter Six, and especially p. 144). As mentioned above, such marriages were termed 'clandestine'. Eventually, in 1753, the Clandestine Marriages Act was passed to stamp out such practices.

March 25th, 1754 to August 31st, 1822

On March 25th, 1754, Lord Hardwicke's Clandestine Marriages Act 1753 came into force. Its aim, as it declared, was to address the 'great mischiefs and inconveniences' that had arisen from the popularity of clandestine marriages. This 1753 Act built on the existing require-ments of the canon law by making certain formalities essential to the validity of future marriages. However, its impact was by no means as drastic as many historians have claimed: contrary to the accounts in many guides to family history, not every failure to comply with the 1753 Act rendered a marriage void.

There were three different ways in which the 1753 Act dealt with the consequences of failing to comply with its directions:

Marriage explicitly stated to be *void*...	Marriage explicitly stated *not* to be void, and therefore *valid*...	Marriage not explicitly stated to be void, and therefore *valid*...
...if not preceded by banns or licence or ...if not celebrated in church	...if parties not resident in parish where banns had been called or for which the licence was obtained	...if not properly registered or ...if registration not attested by two witnesses

Table 4.1 Provisions of the Marriage Act 1753

These are examined in more detail below, along with the possibility of marrying by special licence. The 1753 Act also established various penalties for clergymen who flouted the law, but as our focus is on whether the marriage was valid these will not be discussed here. It is, though, worth remembering that the risk of transportation for fourteen years did act as a serious incentive to clergymen to comply with the requirements of the law.

i. Circumstances in which a marriage would be void

The Act stated that 'all marriages solemnized... without publication of banns, or Licence of Marriage from a Person or Persons having Authority to grant the same first had and obtained, shall be null and void to all Intents and Purposes whatsoever'.

Banns

As well as making either banns or licence essential to the validity of all subsequent marriages, the Act also tightened up the circumstances in which banns could be called. Banns could henceforth only be called on three consecutive Sundays (rather than, as canon law had allowed, on any three consecutive holy days *or* Sundays). If the bride or groom was under the age of 21, it was also possible for parents or guardians to forbid the banns. If an objection was voiced, the result was that the publication of the banns was void, and in the unlikely event that the marriage proceeded nevertheless, it too would be void (see 'Parental consent to marriages by banns', p. 113).

Where the banns were called was important. This had to take place in 'the parish church, or in some publick chapel', and the marriage had to take place in the same church or chapel where the banns had been published. However, it was not possible to invalidate a marriage at a later date on the basis that neither of the parties had been resident in the parish where the banns were called and the marriage solemnized. This meant that the requirement that banns should be published in the parishes where *each* of the parties were resident was effectively directory rather than mandatory, and that the marriage was not invalidated if this had not been done.

Key fact: marrying in a parish other than the one(s) in which the parties were resident did not invalidate a marriage.

How the banns were called was also to prove important. Since the whole purpose of calling the banns was to make the local community aware of the proposed marriage and identify any impediments, having the banns called in a false name would clearly defeat the whole purpose of the Act. Equally, being *too* strict on the names that were used might invalidate whole swathes of marriages, and this was entirely contrary to the policy of the law.

The solutions adopted were sensible and pragmatic. First, it was held that the name in which the banns should be called was the one by which the person in question was usually known in that community. This meant that a marriage would not be annulled simply on the basis that the banns were called in a name slightly different from that bestowed at baptism. It also had the advantage that those passing under a false name could not wriggle out of the marriage at a later stage by revealing their baptismal name. For the family historian, an added significance of this point lies in the variability of surnames at the time and the possible lines of enquiry opened up by the surname used at the time of the marriage. In one case from 1807, for example, the bride used her mother's maiden name as her own surname when she married, and this is a possibility to consider if the usual inquiries have proved fruitless. (This marriage, incidentally, was held to be valid even though the bride was not normally known by her mother's maiden name.)

In fact, only if the name used was one to which the individual had no claim whatsoever, or if a variation had been adopted in order to disguise the fact of the marriage from parents who might otherwise object to it going ahead (see p. 116), would the courts hold that the banns had not been properly called and declare the marriage void. It always needs to be borne in mind that it was up to the person challenging the marriage to show that it was void, rather than for those wishing to uphold the marriage to show that it was valid:

Q. *When examining a banns book, I discovered that when my ancestors married in 1799 the banns were called in the name of 'Joan', but my great-great-great-great-grandmother signed the marriage register as 'Jane'. Was the marriage void as a result?*

A. No. As always, it is important to remember that if a marriage was not challenged at the time, the legal presumption is that it was validly celebrated. Even when a marriage was challenged during the lifetime of the parties, the courts required very strong evidence that the banns had deliberately been called in the wrong name. In a case from 1794, according to the register the banns had been published in the name of 'Fanon', but the groom signed his name as 'Follon'. The court decided that it was more likely that the clergyman had made a mistake in recording the calling of the banns than in actually publishing the banns, and upheld the marriage as valid.

In other words, the fact that banns were so essential to a marriage meant that the courts were very wary of finding that they had not been properly called, and strove wherever possible to find that the formal requirements had been observed. Only if it was clear that a completely false name had been used, or if a more minor variation had been motivated by some fraudulent purpose, would the marriage be held to be void.

Licences

Under the 1753 Act, as under the canon law, it was possible to shorten the waiting time before a marriage by obtaining a licence. The Act attempted to ensure that couples married in the parish where they were resident, stipulating that a licence was only to be granted to solemnise the marriage in the church of the parish or chapelry where at least one of the persons had resided for four weeks. Once a marriage had been celebrated, however, it was not possible to challenge it on the basis that the parties had not in truth resided in the place where the marriage was solemnised. Family historians who find evidence that a marriage by licence was celebrated in a parish where the parties were not resident, or in a different parish to that stated in the licence, must not conclude that the marriage was therefore invalid.

Key fact: marriage by licence in a parish where the parties were not resident still created a valid marriage.

But even if a licence had been obtained, the marriage might yet be void if either of the parties was under the age of 21 and had not obtained parental consent (see p. 117). Again, however, the courts' willingness to presume in favour of the validity of a marriage meant that it was difficult to challenge a marriage on this basis after any lapse of time. It is also important to note that the legislation did not say anything about a marriage being void if the licence was obtained under false pretences:

Q. *I suspect that an ancestor gave a false name when marrying by licence in the late eighteenth century. Was the marriage void?*

A. No. The courts held that it was not essential that the correct names of the parties should be set out in the licence.

Obtaining a licence required a bond to guarantee that the information given as to age and parental consent was true. Don't be misled by the large sums of money mentioned: these were the penalties threatened for false swearing, not the cost of the licence.

The place of celebration

The Act stipulated that banns should be called in 'the parish church, or in some publick chapel, in which publick chapel banns of matrimony have been usually published', and went on to state that 'all marriages solemnized... in any other place than a church or such publick chapel... shall be null and void'. This was intended to ensure that the Act was not evaded through the use of private chapels.

> **Key fact: from March 25th, 1754 until June 30th, 1837, marriages celebrated outside a parish church or chapel (other than by 'special licence') were void.**

Unfortunately, the Act's wording unintentionally limited the valid celebration of marriages by banns to churches and chapels existing at the time of the Act. Nevertheless, family historians who have found an ancestor marrying in a church or chapel built after 1754 can be reassured: legislation was passed in 1781, 1804, 1825, and 1830 to ratify such marriages retrospectively.

ii. Circumstances under which the Act explicitly stated that a marriage would not be void, and was therefore valid

As noted above, the 1753 Act stated that a marriage could not be annulled if the parties were not resident in the parish where banns had been called or for which the licence was obtained. The impact of the 1753 Act on where couples married in practice is considered further in Chapter Six, p. 146.

iii. Circumstances under which the Act made no explicit statement that a marriage would be void, and was therefore valid

The 1753 Act was tightly drafted, and explicitly identified which failures to comply with the law would invalidate a marriage. Despite the assumptions of many popular historians and genealogical guide-books, it was not the case that any failure to comply with the letter of the law would invalidate a marriage, since certain requirements were only directory, and not mandatory:

Registration

For the genealogist, the registration of an ancestor's marriage is the most important part of the ceremony, since without such registration there is no proof that it ever took place. In the eyes of the law, however, registration has never been essential to the validity of a marriage. While the 1753 Act tried to encourage more accurate and careful recording of marriages, there was never any question of a marriage being invalidated simply because the register was not kept as directed. Given the number of registers that did not comply with the statutory requirements, this was just as well.

Q. *My guidebook to family history tells me that under the Marriage Act 1753 marriage registers had to be numbered and ruled in a specific way, otherwise the marriages were invalid. I have found one which was kept in a very haphazard manner: was my ancestor's marriage invalid as a result?*

A. No. The Act did set out how the register should be kept, but sloppy recording had no impact on the validity of the marriages recorded.

Even a failure to register the marriage *altogether* did not render it void, as numerous judges noted when discussing what proof of a marriage was required.

Key fact: in English law, failure to register a marriage has never rendered it invalid.

Witnesses

The Act did not actually stipulate that the marriage be celebrated in the presence of witnesses, only that they should attest its registration. Since, as explained above, deficiencies in registration did not render the marriage void, the lack of witnesses to the registration could have no effect on the validity of the marriage. From a legal point of view, witnesses were ideally individuals who could be called upon to prove that the marriage had taken place in case of a later dispute; but this was a matter on which the law left it to the couple to decide: there were no statutory restrictions on who could act as a witness.

Special licences

The alternative to marrying by banns or licence was to obtain a 'special licence'. Such licences, granted exclusively by the Archbishop of Canterbury himself, allowed a marriage to be celebrated at any time or place. If a couple wished to marry in a private chapel, or in the privacy of their own home, a special licence had to be purchased, at considerable cost. Money alone was not sufficient, however, as in 1759 the Archbishop made it clear that special licences would only be granted to 'Peers, and Peeresses in their own right of Great Britain and Ireland, to their sons and daughters, to Dowager Peeresses, to Privy Councillors, to Judges of his Majesty's Courts in Westminster Hall, to Baronets and Knights and to members of the House of Commons.' Anyone else had to show 'very strong and weighty reasons' in order to be entitled to the privilege of marrying by special licence.

So it is only if your ancestors belonged to the higher echelons of society that you need to consider the possibility that they might have married by special licence. In addition, it was directed that diligent checks should be made as to the parties' status and age, and if there was a risk that either party might be under the age of 21 officials were directed to check that parental consent had been obtained. The option of a special licence was there to permit approved marriages to take place with a degree of privacy, not to enable couples to evade the terms of the Act.

In summary

There was far less scope than commonly portrayed for marriages to be challenged under the 1753 Act. The family historian who has read accounts of widespread invalidity and considers that some minor infraction of the law might have rendered an ancestor's marriage void should be reassured: even in the eighteenth century the approach of the courts was, in the absence of evidence to the contrary, to presume that the formalities had been duly observed and that a marriage was valid.

There is little evidence that individuals had any difficulty in complying with the requirements of the 1753 Act. What did prove problematic, and led eventually to reform, were the provisions relating to parental consent to the marriages of minors (see Chapter

Five, p. 113). And attempts to address the problems these had raised led to a swift series of changes in the law.

September 1st, 1822 to March 25th, 1823

For this short period there were more *directory* requirements, meaning that couples had more rules to contend with, but no longer any *mandatory* requirements, making it less likely that a marriage could later be invalidated. Under the Marriage Act 1822, no licence was to be granted unless both parties swore on oath that they were, and believed the other to be, at least 21 years of age. In addition, each was required to provide supporting evidence: either an extract from the register of baptism (which had to be sworn on oath by a third party to be a true extract) or, if the register could not be found, someone to swear on oath that the individual in question was of age and to provide grounds for believing this to be the case. If either was under the age of 21, further precautions were taken to ensure that parental consent had truly been given. Finally, both had to swear as to their place of residence during the preceding four weeks.

Similarly detailed requirements were also included for marriages by banns: couples had to deliver an affidavit as to their names, ages and places of residence to the clergyman before the banns were published.

Anybody wilfully giving false evidence, either to obtain a licence or to the clergyman responsible for calling the banns, would be committing perjury and vulnerable to punishment. In addition, anybody who obtained a licence by giving false information would be committing a felony and liable to transportation for life. But those rare souls who obtained a licence by deception and who were subsequently transported to the colonies would at least have the consolation that their marriage would be legally valid: the 1822 Act explicitly stated that a marriage could not be challenged on the basis of non-compliance after it had taken place.

March 26th, 1823 to October 31st, 1823

The level of detail provided by licences and affidavits under the 1822 Act might be a dream for the family historian, but they were a nightmare for those responsible for the administration of the law.

Within a few months it was noted in Parliament that the oaths had been found to be 'unnecessary and vexatious'. The 1822 Act was repealed, and between the above dates the 1753 Act was restored.

November 1st, 1823 to June 30th, 1837

But within a few months there was yet another new Act, the Marriage Act 1823. This struck a compromise between the potential invalidity of marriages caused by the 1753 Act and the bureaucratic declarations required by the 1822 Act. It tightened up the formalities required in a number of respects, and at the same time established the basic rule (which still applies today) that a marriage would only be void if the couple 'knowingly and wilfully' failed to comply with certain specified requirements.

> **Key fact: the Marriage Act 1823 introduced the concept that only 'knowingly and wilfully' failing to comply with the law could render a marriage invalid.**

Q. *I have discovered that my great-great-great-grandmother married in the 1830s, calling herself a spinster and using a different Christian name. In fact, she was already married at the time the banns were called, although her first husband conveniently died just before the wedding. Was the marriage void because of this?*

A. Not unless the name had been adopted for the purposes of deception or concealment *and* the second husband had been aware of the facts at the time of the wedding. In a similar case from 1837, *Wright v Elwood*, the court held that the use of the name 'Emma' rather than 'Amelia' was immaterial, these being essentially the same name. In any event, since the husband's case was that he had been deceived, this in itself was proof that he did not know that a different name had been used. As for the banns being called while your ancestor was still married to somebody else, so long as nobody raised before the ceremony it would not have prevented the marriage going ahead.

Provision was made for banns to be called in churches and chapels built after the 1823 Act was passed, rather than only those already existing. No formal affidavits as to the parties' particulars were required, but notice of their true names and abode was to be given to the clergyman. An additional requirement was that banns would have to be republished if the marriage did not take place within three months of their first being called. In practical terms, this gave rise to the possibility that family historians might today come across more than one set of banns for the same ancestors.

Q. *I have discovered that my ancestors married three-and-a-half months after the banns were published. Does this mean that the marriage was void?*

A. Not unless they married knowing that the banns had lapsed and should have been called again. In a case from 1867 the court gave a couple in a similar situation the benefit of the doubt and upheld the marriage.

With regard to marriage by licence, the minimum residence period was reduced from four weeks to 15 days by the 1823 Act. A licence could be granted after a simple oath by just one of the parties as to their residence and the lack of impediments to the marriage and, if either was under 21, that parental consent had been given.

Once again, most of these requirements were directory. A marriage was only void if the couple had 'knowingly and wilfully' failed to marry in a church or public chapel, or married without due publication of banns or obtaining a licence, or knowing that the person solemnizing the marriage was not in holy orders. The first two of these reiterated the requirements of the 1753 Act, but the last was an innovation. Litigation in 1820 had established that a marriage could not be challenged on the sole basis that the person officiating over the ceremony was not in fact properly ordained; the new provision ensured that a marriage would be void only if the parties knew at the time of the marriage that the clergyman had not been properly ordained.

Q. *I have discovered a licence for my ancestors' marriage dated the day after the marriage took place in 1830! Presumably such a marriage must have been void?*

A. Not necessarily: it depends on whether *both* the bride and groom knew that the licence had not been obtained before the wedding. In *Greaves v Greaves* (1874), the bride had been blissfully unaware that her husband had only secured the licence the day after the wedding, and the marriage was upheld. As always, if the marriage was not challenged during your ancestors' lifetimes, it should be presumed to be legally valid.

The Marriage Act 1836: from July 1st, 1837 to the present day

The Marriage Act 1836 left Anglican marriages largely untouched. Couples now had the novel choice of using the new civil preliminaries, but retained the possibility of marrying after banns, licence, or special licence. In practice, banns continued to be far and away the most popular preliminary, followed by licence, civil preliminaries, and a tiny number of special licences.

Of more fundamental interest to the family historian is the effect of the provisions of the Civil Registration Act 1836, relating to the registration of marriages. From July 1st, 1837, Church of England clergy were under an obligation to send certified copies of all marriages celebrated in their church to the superintendent registrar of the district every quarter. The registrar would then send copies to the General Register Office so that for the first time there would be a centrally held record of the marriage rather than simply an entry in a parish register.

The Registrar General wrote to all members of the clergy to remind them of their obligations under the Act and to extol the advantages of having a simple and readily accessible means of proving that a marriage had taken place. He expressed his confidence that this consideration would be sufficient motivation for a clergyman to comply with the new civil duties, 'especially when he feels that by neglecting to perform them, he may inflict an injury he knows not how serious, on the descendants of those who have received at his hands the holy ordinance of marriage.' The Registrar General presumably had in mind those descendants who might need to prove the marriage for legal purposes, rather than those tracing their family tree, but genealogists nonetheless have much cause to be grateful for the more systematic methods of registration adopted from 1837. Nonetheless, not all marriages that were recorded in the parish registers found their way into the central registers, and errors in transcription mean that the names of the parties are not always correctly indexed. Once again, it needs to be emphasised that a failure to find a marriage record should not be taken as evidence that the couple in question never married.

Subsequent changes may be briefly noted. As the Church of England lost its almost exclusive monopoly on matrimony, it could afford to obtain exemptions from the celebration of certain types of marriage. When legislation was passed in 1857 allowing judicial divorce for the first time, a clause was included to the effect that no Anglican clergyman could be compelled to solemnize the remarriage of anybody whose former marriage had been dissolved because of his or her adultery. When the grounds for divorce were extended to encompass cruelty and desertion, this exemption was amended to allow a clergyman to refuse to marry any divorced person, and this remains the case today.

Key fact: since 1857 Anglican clergymen have been able to refuse to solemnise the marriage of a divorced person.

Similar exemptions were included when marriages within the formerly prohibited degrees became possible.

In 1949, another Marriage Act consolidated the law. This reiterated the grounds set out in the 1823 Act as to when a marriage may be annulled and (with a few amendments unlikely to worry the current generation of genealogists) continues to govern this area of law.

CIVIL MARRIAGES

The history of civil marriage has rather less continuity than that of Anglican weddings. Apart from a brief period under the Commonwealth, it was not until 1837 that it was possible to marry in a civil ceremony.

September 29th, 1653 to 1660

During the Commonwealth, the most cherished institutions in England and Wales were turned upside down. It might seem odd that the most religiously inspired regime ever to rule over these lands should introduce civil marriage, but it was in fact consistent with the Puritans' notion that God was everywhere, and with their rejection of the allegedly 'popish' ceremonies associated with Anglican marriage. While the Marriage Act 1653 stipulated that a marriage had to take place before a local Justice of the Peace, the prescribed vows were far from secular in nature:

> 'I, A.B. do here in the presence of God the searcher of all hearts, take thee C.D. for my wedded Wife; and do also in the presence of God, and before these witnesses, promise to be unto thee a loving and faithful Husband.'

The bride made an identical vow, save that she also promised to be 'obedient'. Nor did the new civil mode of marrying do away with the old procedures entirely. Information about those intending to marry was still to be published on three Sundays, after morning service (or 'exercise' in the language of the Puritans) in 'the publique Meeting-place commonly called the Church or Chappel'. As an alternative, the necessary information could be published in the Market-place on three market days.

For the family historian the main provisions of interest for this period are those relating to registration. Recording the marriage was the role of the Register, elected by the local ratepayers and approved by the Justice of the Peace. Since the Register could be a local clergyman, and since small parishes could share a Register, the result was that some parishes recorded no marriages at all for this period while others saw a dramatic increase solely because it was their clergyman who was responsible for keeping the book in which all marriages for the district were recorded.

The 1653 Act declared forthrightly that after September 29th, 1653 no other form of marriage would be valid, but only four years later Parliament backtracked and omitted this clause. Precisely what other marriages would be permitted was never put to the test and was rendered academic by the Restoration in 1660. It was, however, felt that legislation was needed to confirm the validity of marriages celebrated before justices of the peace in the previous two troubled decades—an indication of just how novel the idea of marrying other than before a clergyman had been.

July 1st, 1837 to the present day

When civil marriage was introduced by the Marriage Act 1836, it was of a very different kind to Cromwell's puritanical but godly rite. The 1836 Act provided that persons could marry 'at the Office and in the Presence of the Superintendent Registrar and some Registrar of the District', what today we would call a 'register office'. The vows that had to be made were entirely secular in nature, simply involving a declaration that there was no impediment to the marriage and calling upon those present to witness that each took the other to be their 'lawful wedded' spouse.

Before so doing, they had to have complied with one of the two new forms of civil preliminaries introduced by the Act, which mirrored the church options of banns and licence. The civil equivalent of banns involved notice of the marriage being given to the superintendent registrar of the district where each party had resided for the previous seven days, and the marriage notices being read out at weekly meetings of Poor Law Guardians on three successive occasions. The more expensive licence, which cost £3 and reduced the waiting period, could be obtained from the superintendent registrar. Sadly, the survival of these records has been patchy, but the centralised system of registration introduced by the Act means that there should be some record of any marriage celebrated after July 1st, 1837.

The provisions of the 1836 Act were even more detailed and bureaucratic provisions than those of its predecessors (even specifying the different colours of the ink to be used when issuing certificates for marriages by licence and marriages without licence). The attentive reader will not be surprised to learn that such specifications were merely directory. As with previous legislation, the 1836 Act had adopted a mix of directory and mandatory requirements, and those relevant to civil marriages are summarized in Table 4.2 below:

Marriage explicitly stated to be *void*...	Marriage explicitly stated *not* to be void, and therefore *valid*...	Marriage not explicitly stated to be void, and therefore *valid*...
...if parties knowingly and wilfully married without due notice or without a licence/certificate having been duly issued or ...if parties knowingly and wilfully married in a place other than that specified or ...if parties knowingly and wilfully married in the absence of the registrar	...if parties not resident in the registration district stated in the notice of marriage or ...if any person whose consent was required had in fact not consented	...if the marriage was not properly registered or ...if the registration was not attested by two witnesses

Table 4.2 Provisions of the Marriage Act 1836 relating to civil marriage

Q. *When my great-grandmother married in a civil ceremony in 1900, she gave a false name to the registrar. I've found letters between her and my great-grandfather indicating that they planned this to prevent the marriage coming to the attention of her father, who disapproved of the match. Did this count as 'knowingly and wilfully' marrying without complying with the stipulated preliminaries?*

A. No. If the couple were marrying in a *civil* ceremony, the inaccuracy of any details in the notice given to the registrar did not invalidate the marriage, whether the marriage was preceded by notice or licence. If they had married by banns, however, the marriage would have been void in this situation.

The take-up of the new option of civil marriage does not suggest any great pent-up demand for non-Anglican marriages. In 1838, the first year for which figures are available, only 1,093 couples—just over 1 per cent of the total—married in a civil wedding. No doubt the association with the Poor Law was off-putting, and discontent with this procedure led to a minor change in 1856: notices of marriage were no longer to be read out at meetings of Poor Law Guardians but simply posted up outside the local register office, a practice that still occurs today. The number and proportion of civil marriages continued to rise slowly, reaching 15 per cent by 1900.

There was, however, a considerable amount of local variation. For the first 50 years after the passage of the 1836 Act, civil marriage was most popular in Wales (especially Monmouthshire, where it was consistently two to three times the national average), the north of England, and the south-west. It would seem that one's occupation was a key determinant of whether or not one married in a civil ceremony, with this option being particularly popular in mining communities.

The refusal of many Anglican clergy to conduct the remarriages of people who had been divorced contributed to the growing popularity of civil marriages in the twentieth century. Even so, it was not until the 1970s that the number of civil marriages exceeded those celebrated according to religious rites, and then only temporarily. Since 1995, by contrast, the civil marriage has become the norm, now accounting for over two-thirds of all marriages. This upsurge in popularity is down to the range of places where one can now legally marry: the 1994 Marriage Act allowed for civil weddings on 'approved premises', and since then numerous hotels, castles, and stately homes have been approved. The family historians of the future may be able to make deductions about the predilections and pastimes of nowadays from the places we choose to marry, be it the changing rooms of Burnley Football Club, the London Eye, or a Tesco Extra store in Cardiff.

Non-Anglican religious marriages

The key shift in how marriages have been celebrated since 1600 has been from exclusively Anglican to largely civil. But what of those who might have wished to be married according to the rites of other faiths or denominations? Some groups, as we shall see, conducted their own marriages even when there were serious legal doubts as to their validity, while others only did so when expressly permitted to do so by legislation. Religious belief can be highly nuanced, and a preference for the doctrine of a particular denomination did not mean that the individuals concerned had theological objections to the idea of marriage in the Anglican Church, still less that they rejected the option of marrying according to its forms altogether when that was the only way permitted.

These differences in practice, and in the way different ceremonies have been regarded by the law, make it convenient to consider each denomination in turn. (Since the Marriage Act 1836 applies to all such marriages, a summary of its key points and the limited grounds that render a marriage void can be found at the end of the section.)

Catholic marriages

Before March 25th, 1754

In the wake of the Gunpowder Plot of 1605, action was taken to try to ensure that the Catholic population was 'integrated' into the mainstream. The expressively titled 1606 'Act to prevent and avoid Dangers which grow by Popish Recusants' required Catholics to be baptised, married and buried in their Anglican parish church, with failure to do so resulting in the loss of property rights. However, the Act did not specifically state that marriages celebrated by Catholic priests would be void, and in the early seventeenth century some legal recognition was accorded to marriages celebrated by Catholic priests who had been lawfully ordained during the reign of the Catholic Queen Mary (1553-58) and who were thus regarded as having the authority to solemnize marriages.

By the late seventeenth century this had ceased to be a possibility, and legislation passed in 1694 referred to Catholic marriages as merely 'pretended' marriages. In a couple of cases, recognition seems to have been given to marriages celebrated by Catholic priests in the London embassies of Catholic countries, but in other cases it was noted that a Catholic marriage was not regarded as being on the same footing as an Anglican one. So Catholic couples who married solely according to their own rites might be punished by the church courts for fornication and denied the usual matrimonial remedies in law.

Key fact: before March 25th, 1754, a Catholic marriage did not have the same legal effect as an Anglican marriage.

Even before March 25th, 1754, therefore, if a record survives of an ancestor marrying in a Catholic ceremony it is worth checking whether there was an additional Anglican ceremony.

March 25th, 1754 to June 30th, 1837

After March 25th, 1754, Catholics almost invariably went through two ceremonies, to fulfil the demands of both faith and law (see the case-study on Coughton Court, below). The scruples of those Catholics who had a principled objection to participating in the religious rites of the Anglican Church were soothed by the fact that compliance could be regarded as a civil requirement rather than a religious act, and there was indeed a formal papal sanction for obeying the law in this respect. This aside, it should not be assumed that Catholic couples regarded the Anglican ceremony as a meaningless legal requirement, as the diary entry of one bride illustrates. The Catholic ceremony having taken place early in the morning:

> 'We had but just time to breakfast, and then I had to dress for the second [i.e., Anglican] marriage—my bridal array consisted of a white satin underdress and a patent net over it, with a long veil… my heart beat when we entered the church, nor could I go thro' the second ceremony without feeling even more affected.'
>
> *The Wynne Diaries* (OUP, 1982), p. 468

The practice of elite Catholics seems to have been to marry first in the Anglican Church and then according to the Catholic rite. By contrast, classes whose behaviour was less subject to scrutiny might prefer to have the Catholic ceremony first, and the Anglican second.

The findings from Coughton Court (below) show the importance that was attached both to a legally binding marriage and to religious conscience: the former was satisfied by the Anglican ceremony, the latter by having the legally invalid Catholic ceremony first.

By the 1830s, however, the huge expansion of the Catholic population, largely as a result of immigration, had led to concerns

Catholic Marriages at Coughton Court: A Case-Study in Catholic Conformity

Between 1758 and 1795, 93 couples married in a Catholic ceremony at the Catholic stronghold of Coughton Court in Warwickshire. Every single one also went through an Anglican ceremony. But where and when should the family historian look for such marriages?

Most of those who went through a Catholic ceremony at Coughton Court do not appear to have been resident in the parish of Coughton. Of the 93, 31 married in the nearby Anglican parish church of Coughton with Sambourne; 51 married in a different parish, specified in the Catholic register; six married in a parish other than that stated in the Catholic register as their home parish; and in the remaining five the absence of details for one or both parties made it impossible to ascertain whether or not the parties had married in a parish where one of them was resident.

Given the paucity of places where Catholic marriages could be celebrated (there was the need, after all, for a Catholic priest, at a time when they were few in number in England), it was understandable that some couples had travelled some distance. While for 70 couples there was only 5 kilometres or less between Coughton Court and the Anglican church where they were legally wed, a further 19 travelled between 6 and 15 kilometres, and the remaining 6 anything up to 34 kilometres (21 miles).

The favoured option was for the Catholic ceremony to take place on a Sunday—presumably when the couple attended Mass—and for the Anglican marriage to take place the day after. In only 5 cases was it clear that the Anglican ceremony had *preceded* the Catholic. This pattern did not vary even when one party to the marriage was Protestant, as was the case for at least one-third of the couples, nor did the pattern here depend on whether it was the husband or wife who was Catholic.

that many Irish Catholic couples were not observing the need for an Anglican ceremony. This was one of the factors leading to reform of the law in 1836, and to Catholic marriages being based on a secure legal foundation for the first time since the sixteenth century.

July 1st, 1837 to present

Under the Marriage Act 1836 a very clear procedure was laid down for such marriages. They had to be preceded by civil preliminaries (see p. 91) and take place in a certified place of worship that had been specifically registered for the solemnization of marriage (a process which required an application with the signatures of twenty house-holders whose usual place of worship it was). By the end of 1838, 197 Roman Catholic places of worship had been registered for marriage. Their distribution across the country was, however, very uneven: by the end of 1845, when the total number had risen to 301, almost a quarter were to be found in Lancashire alone, while Yorkshire accounted for a further 13%; Cambridgeshire, meanwhile, had none. While legislation in 1840 made it possible to marry in a non-Anglican religious ceremony outside one's district of residence, in the nearest registered chapel of one's own denomination, some Catholics clearly had further to travel than others.

Under the 1836 Act, the exact form of the Catholic ceremony had been left to the discretion of the religious authorities, but state super-vision was ensured by the requirement that the ceremony take place in the presence of a civil registrar. While legislation passed in 1898 allowed religious organisations to appoint an authorised person to replace the registrar, Catholic churches did not immediately avail themselves of this option and to this day often continue to have a civil registrar present at marriage ceremonies.

The number of Catholic marriages grew very slowly over the course of the nineteenth century; by 1900, when there were over 300,000 weddings in total, only 10,000 or so were celebrated according to Catholic rites. That number rose to some 45,000 in 1968, but has since fallen back to a lower level even than in 1900.

Protestant dissenters

Before March 25th, 1754

Baptists, Independents and Presbyterians

Genealogists whose ancestors were dissenters might be surprised to find their marriages recorded in the parish register, but this was in fact the norm. While Presbyterian and Independent ideas about how marriage should be celebrated had a significant influence on the law of marriage during the 1640s and 1650s, after the Restoration in 1660 all the evidence suggests that the overwhelming majority of dissenters married in the Church of England (with the exception of members of the Society of Friends, whose practices are considered further below).

Only a handful of dissenting congregations' marriage registers can be traced to this period, far lower than the number of dissenting congregations would lead one to expect had they been in the habit of performing marriages. Of the 505 Presbyterian, Baptist or Independent congregations founded prior to 1754, only eight produced marriage registers relating to that period when requested by an official commission in 1838. These eight recorded fewer than 200 marriages between them, over a period of more than one hundred years. Set this against the fact that the end of the seventeenth century saw the numbers of dissenters peak at an estimated 300,000, and it is clear that most dissenters were clearly not marrying in their own chapels according to their own rites. Moreover, in one of the eight—the Independent chapel in Dorking—it was clear that the register was simply recording the marriages of members of the congregation which had taken place in the Anglican parish church.

> **Key fact: both before and after 1754, through to the Marriage Act 1836, marriage in the Anglican Church was the norm for dissenting Protestants.**

For family historians who have traced a record of an ancestor's marriage in a Presbyterian, Baptist or Independent chapel, therefore, it is worth checking the Anglican registers as well. But the more likely situation is that the only record of a marriage between dissenters is an Anglican one: set against the very rare examples of dissenters marrying in their own chapels but not in church is the abundant evidence that the overwhelming majority married in the Church of England. This observation has wider implications for the thorough genealogist: it should not be assumed that a dissenting ancestor was any less committed to their faith just because they married in the Anglican Church; conversely, it should be borne in mind that finding an Anglican marriage for an ancestor does not mean that they were not a regular chapel-going dissenter.

Moravians

The same is true of the Moravian churches that were established in England in the early eighteenth century. The Protestant Moravian Church, which had its origins in medieval Bohemia, had parallels with the emerging evangelical movement of this time, with Moravians regarding themselves as being part of, rather than an alternative to, the Church of England. The evidence accordingly suggests that they married in the Church of England: while there is a surviving pre-1754 register for the Moravian church in Bedford, the marriages it recorded actually took place in the Church of England—a reminder of the need to check exactly what any particular record is telling us).

Methodists

Similarly, early Methodists regarded themselves as part of the Church of England and (with very occasional exceptions) had no objection to marrying according to its forms.

March 25th, 1754 to June 30th, 1837

The passage of the Marriage Act 1753 accordingly had little impact on these groups, who continued to marry in the Church of England as before. The occasional dissenting registers that do record marriages after March 25th, 1754 are, just as before, merely noting ones that took place in the Anglican Church.

July 1st, 1837 to the present day

Under the Marriage Act 1836, Protestant dissenters acquired the right to marry according to their own rites. Such marriages had to be preceded by civil preliminaries (see p. 91), and, as was the case with Catholics, the place of celebration had to be registered for the purposes of marriage. In 1838, Independents led the list of those whose places of worship had been registered, with 547 out of 1,257. Baptists were in second place, with 246 places registered, while the Unitarians had 73, the Presbyterians 36 and the Moravians just one.

Since most of these registrations had only taken place the previous year, it is perhaps unsurprising that in 1838 fewer than 3,000 couples married in a non-Anglican religious ceremony. Most dissenting denominations had no history of conducting their own marriages, and it took some time for the idea to be accepted.

Q. *From all the evidence, my ancestor was a Wesleyan Methodist, but it seems that he married in the Church of England in 1845. Why might he have done so?*

A. In the first half of the nineteenth century, there was not the same stark distinction between church and chapel as later emerged, and many dissenters continued to marry in the Anglican Church. The proportion of Wesleyan Methodists' places of worship that were registered for marriage was significantly lower than that for other denominations, and it was perfectly normal for them to marry in church.

Q. *I have discovered that my ancestors married in a Baptist chapel in 1850 and then again in the Church of England! Surely there were no longer any doubts about the validity of such dissenting marriages in this period?*

A. Although the 1836 Act had explicitly stated that a non-Anglican marriage according to the methods set out would have exactly the same status as one celebrated in the Church of England, not all Anglican clergy shared this view. Some clergymen insisted that marriage was a sacred rite that should still be celebrated according to the ceremonies of the Church of England, regardless of the range of options now available, and persuaded their dissenting parishioners to go through a second ceremony. Other dissenters wanted an additional blessing on their union.

The possibility of having a free-standing blessing, rather than a second marriage, was only introduced by the Marriage and Registration Amendment Act 1856. This allowed for a religious service to be held after a civil ceremony but emphasized that 'nothing in the Reading or Celebration of such service shall be held to supersede or invalidate [the Register Office wedding]; nor shall such Reading or Celebration be entered as a Marriage.'

As with civil and Catholic marriages, there were considerable local variations to dissenting marriages. By the end of the nineteenth century, Northumberland contained almost one-fifth of the Presbyterian churches in England and Wales that were registered for marriage, reflecting the distinctive heritage of this border region. The biggest concentration of Congregationalist and Baptist chapels was to be found in South Wales, while North Wales was home to the largest number of Calvinistic Methodist chapels. In fact, across Wales the number of non-Anglican churches and chapels registered for marriage considerably outnumbered those of the Anglican Church. The reverse was true in southern England, with the exceptions of London and Middlesex. As one moved north, however, the pattern changed, with Staffordshire, Derbyshire, Cheshire, the West Riding and Durham all containing more non-Anglican places of worship where one could marry than Anglican ones. Lancashire, however, topped the list, with more than twice as many non-Anglican places of worship as Anglican ones. These regional variations need to be borne in mind when evaluating the likelihood of an ancestor being found in the Anglican parish registers in any given county during this period (for further detail see Table 4.5, p. 108).

A further requirement of the 1836 Act was that a non-Anglican marriage on registered religious premises had to take place in the presence of a civil registrar. This was a source of grievance to some, and when in 1898 it became possible for an authorised person to be appointed to carry out this role it was the Methodists who were most keen on establishing their own authority, with the Wesleyans alone accounting for almost half of those who appointed an authorised person to replace the registrar, and other Methodist denominations for a further one-sixth.

Marriage explicitly stated to be *void*...	Marriage explicitly stated *not* to be void, and therefore *valid*...	Marriage not explicitly stated to be void, and therefore *valid*...
...if parties knowingly and wilfully married without due notice or without a licence/certificate having been duly issued or ...if parties knowingly and wilfully married in a place other than that specified or ...if parties knowingly and wilfully married in the absence of the registrar, or (after 1898) other authorised person	...if parties not resident in the registration district stated in the notice of marriage or ...if any person whose consent was required had in fact not consented or ...if the building where the marriage had been solemnized had not been certified as a place of worship or was not the usual place of worship of either of the parties	...if the marriage was not properly registered or ...if the registration was not attested by two witnesses

Table 4.3 Provisions of the Marriage Act 1836 relating to non-Anglican religious marriages other than those of Jews and Quakers, summarizing the circumstances in which such a marriage may be void for failing to comply with the legal requirements

Jewish marriages

Before March 25th, 1754

For centuries the Jewish community in England and Wales barely existed, since their expulsion in 1290. Even when permitted to return, from the 1650s onwards, their numbers remained low. On the rare occasions when Jewish marriages came before a court, the view would seem to have been that their validity (or otherwise) should be determined by Jewish law, although in the event this was never explicitly decided.

March 25th, 1754 to June 30th, 1837

This remained the case even after the Marriage Act 1753. As with the Quakers (see below), the 1753 Act had not declared Jewish marriages to be valid, merely that the Act did not extend to them. In the event, it was not until the 1790s that any English court had occasion to pronounce on the validity of a Jewish marriage. Evidence was taken from experts in Jewish law and applied to the facts of the case just as they would apply the laws of a foreign country in determining the validity of a marriage celebrated overseas.

July 1st, 1837 to the present day

The Marriage Act 1836 was much more explicit as to the status of Jewish (and Quaker) marriages than the 1753 Act had been, stating that members of these groups 'may continue to contract and solemnise marriage' according to their own usages, and that 'every such marriage is hereby declared and confirmed good in law'. Under the Act, Jewish couples were required to comply with the new civil preliminaries, and under the Civil Registration Act of the same year the synagogue was required to send copies of the marriage register to the registrar of the district. Otherwise, the solemnisation of Jewish marriages was left to their own religious authorities, and the presence of a registrar was not required.

A Jewish marriage could, however, be declared void by an English court on the basis that it had not been performed in accordance with Jewish law. For this reason, the 1836 Act retained the requirement that only couples who were *both* of the Jewish faith could marry according to these forms. If one spouse was of a different faith, or indeed no faith, then they would either have to marry in the Church of England or take advantage of the new option of civil marriage. This requirement has added to the mistaken belief that Jews and Gentiles could not legally intermarry (see p. 68).

The Society of Friends (Quakers)

Before March 25th, 1754

Unlike other seventeenth-century Protestant dissenters, the Quakers did develop their own distinct marriage practices. Quaker registers contain 203 marriages for the period 1647-59 alone, and 17,823 by 1749, despite the fact that there were far fewer members of the Society of Friends than there were Presbyterian, Independents or Baptists.

The Quaker process of marriage was both very simple (in that the actual marriage consisted of nothing more than an exchange of vows before the assembled meeting) and very demanding (in that preliminary investigations were carried out by fellow Quakers as to whether the pair could and should marry). But it was also far from certain what the legal status of such marriages was. The Quakers' own accounts record numerous disputes over the decades, and in the 1690s Parliament even referred to their marriages as 'pretended' (just as it did those of Catholics). Quakers could find themselves in the church courts for fornication on the basis that they were not properly married, and they were unable to access the remedies against marital breakdown that were available in those courts.

Key fact: before March 25th, 1754, Quaker marriages were not regarded as valid by the church courts.

Such doubts mean that family historians with Quaker ancestors might well find them marrying in the Anglican Church, although this in turn could lead to them being disowned by their co-religionists and shut out of the fellowship of the Society.

March 25th, 1754 to June 30th, 1837

Doubts as to the validity of Quaker marriages continued even after 1754. The 1753 Act had not declared such marriages valid, merely that the Act did not cover them, and the number of 'disownments' for being married in the Anglican Church actually increased in the wake of the Act. As late as 1794 it was pointed out during litigation that the validity of Quaker marriages had never been formally decided, and contemporaries continued to express doubts about their validity.

Key fact: despite their exemption from the 1753 Act, the status of Quaker marriages remained uncertain until the nineteenth century.

Only after the case of *Dalrymple v Dalrymple* in 1811, when Sir William Scott mistakenly held that an exchange of consent had constituted a valid marriage in England and Wales prior to 1754, do we find courts assuming that Quaker marriages were valid.

July 1st, 1837 to the present day

The Marriage Act 1836 brought Quaker marriages within the sphere of legal regulation, requiring them to comply with civil preliminaries and registration but otherwise leaving the form, timing and place of the marriage up to the Quakers themselves. The number recorded in the first year of the Act's operation was, nevertheless, much lower than in the Quakers' heyday, with only 76 taking place.

For the sake of certainty, further legislation was passed in 1847 to validate Quaker marriages that had taken place prior to the Marriage Act 1836. So while there may have been doubts about the validity of Quaker marriages at the time that they were celebrated from the late 1640s to the early nineteenth century, the key point for the family historian is that these marriages would have been regarded as valid had there been any later challenge.

Key fact: Quaker marriages celebrated before July 1st, 1837 were given retrospective validity in 1847.

As a final note, just as with Jewish marriages (see p. 103) the 1836 Act retained the requirement that only couples who were *both* Quakers could marry in a Quaker ceremony. In 1872, however, this restriction was relaxed. In its place was substituted a requirement that an officer of the Society of Friends must issue a certificate confirming that any bride or groom who was not a member of the Society was authorised to be married in accordance with their usages.

Table 4.4 sets out the circumstances in which a Jewish or Quaker marriage might be void for failing to comply with the requirements of the 1836 Act:

Marriage explicitly stated to be *void*...	Marriage explicitly stated *not* to be void, and therefore *valid*...	Marriage not explicitly stated to be void, and therefore *valid*...
...if parties knowingly and wilfully married without due notice or without a licence/certificate having been duly issued	...if parties not resident in the registration district stated in the notice of marriage or ...if any person whose consent was required had in fact not consented	...if the marriage was not properly registered or ...if the registration was not attested by two witnesses

Table 4.4 Provisions of the Marriage Act 1836 relating to Jewish or Quaker marriages

FURTHER READING

Anderson, O. 'The Incidence of Civil Marriage in Victorian England and Wales' (1975) 69 *Past & Present* 50

Cretney, S. *Family Law in the Twentieth Century: A History* (Oxford University Press, 2003), ch. 1

Haskey, J. 'Marriage Rites: Trends in Marriages by Manner of Solemnisation and Denomination in England and Wales, 1841 to 2012', in Miles, Mody, and Probert (eds) *Marriage Rites & Rights* (Hart, 2015)

On trends in religious observance
Gilbert, A. *Religion and Society in Industrial England: Church, Chapel and Social Change, 1740-1914* (Longman, 1976)

Rosman, D. *The Evolution of the English Churches, 1500-2000* (Cambridge University Press, 2003)

Spaeth, D. *The Church in an Age of Danger: Parsons and Parishioners 1660-1740* (Cambridge University Press, 2000)

On Catholics
Arkell, VTJ. 'An Enquiry into the Frequency of the Parochial Registration of Catholics in a Seventeenth-Century Warwickshire Parish' (1972) 9 *Local Population Studies* 23

Aveling, DH. 'The Marriages of Catholic Recusants, 1559-1642' (1963) 14 *Journal of Ecclesiastical History* 68

Bossy, J. *The English Catholic Community, 1570-1850* (Darton, Longman & Todd, 1975)

Leys, MDR. *Catholics in England, 1559-1829: A Social History* (Longmans, Green and Co Ltd, 1961)

Probert R. and D'Arcy-Brown, L. 'Catholics and the Clandestine Marriages Act of 1753' (2008) *Local Population Studies* 78

On Protestant dissenters
Manning, BL. *The Protestant Dissenting Deputies* (Cambridge University Press, 1952)

Watts, MR. *The Dissenters: From the Reformation to the French Revolution* (Clarendon Press, 1978)

On Methodists
Hempton, D. *The Religion of the People: Methodism and Popular Religion c. 1750-1900* (Routledge, 1996)

Rack, HD. '"But Lord, let it be Betsy!" Love and Marriage in Early Methodism' (2001) 53 *Proceedings of the Wesley Historical Society* 1

On Quakers
Tual, J. 'Sexual Equality and Conjugal Harmony: The Way to Celestial Bliss. A View of Early Quaker Matrimony' (1988) 55 *Journal of the Friends Historical Society* 161

Vann, RT. *The Social Development of English Quakerism, 1655-1755* (Harvard University Press, 1969)

On Jews
Henriques, HSQ. *The Jews and the English Law* (J. Jacobs, 1908)

Wolf, L. 'Crypto-Jews under the Commonwealth' (1893-4) I *Transactions of the Jewish Historical Society of England* 55.

	London	South East	South Mids	East	South West	West Mids	North Mids	North West	Yorks	North	Wales	Avge
Anglican	72.96	73.50	77.30	78.41	64.98	75.69	70.97	62.57	70.38	56.49	32.67	66.90
Catholic	3.49	1.63	1.05	1.37	2.75	2.45	1.60	9.86	4.31	7.58	2.66	3.52
Civil	16.06	15.26	10.74	10.62	15.95	12.56	12.76	11.10	10.17	22.50	37.59	15.94
Jewish	2.85	0.03	>0.01	>0.01	0.01	0.16	0.03	0.50	0.46	0.19	0.12	0.4
Quaker	0.02	0.04	0.03	0.04	0.03	0.05	>0.01	0.02	0.04	0.08	0	0.03
Other Christian	4.62	9.54	10.88	9.56	16.28	9.09	14.63	15.95	14.64	13.16	26.96	13.21

Table 4.5 Marriages in England and Wales in 1899, by type and denomination (%) (see p. 101) (source: *62nd Annual Report of the Registrar General, 1900*)

As the table shows, by the end of the nineteenth century the likelihood of an ancestor marrying in any particular form varied to a considerable degree depending on where in the country they lived.

❦ 5 ❦

WHEN

AGE AT MARRIAGE
THE TIMING OF THE MARRIAGE
CHOOSING A DATE

The timing of marriage in a person's life, unlike other vital events such as birth and death, is culturally determined. Whether individuals marry for the first time in childhood, in their early teens, twenties, thirties, or later tells us much about the society in question and the way in which marriage is regarded. The issue is of course a complex one: on the one hand, disapproval of sex before marriage is likely to lead to men and women wanting to marry at earlier ages; on the other hand, people's wishes might be constrained by both legal and practical constraints—did they need parental consent in order to marry, and could they afford to set up home together without parental support?

Similarly, over the centuries different months, days and hours have been popular at different times and for different reasons. While some of these seasonal differences have been influenced by legal considerations, the law has never taken the drastic step of invalidating marriages simply because they took place at one time of the year, the week or the day rather than another.

Key fact: the time and date at which a marriage took place has never by itself had the legal effect of rendering it invalid.

This chapter will look first at the age when individuals *could* marry (with or without parental consent), and then at when couples *did* marry (in terms of both their age and the stage of their relationship). It closes by considering the factors governing the choice of different seasons, days, and hours of the day for weddings.

Age at marriage

The age at which a person could legally marry has varied over time, with differing requirements over parental consent depending on the parties' ages. We will deal first with the minimum age at which a person could marry, and then with the issue of parental consent.

Minimum age

The Church of England's canon law presumed that a person was capable of marrying once they had reached the nominal age of puberty—twelve for girls and fourteen for boys: the primary stated aim of marriage was, after all, procreation, and a marriage had in theory to be capable of fruitful consummation.

But a legal presumption is, by its very nature, capable of being rebutted. People over the specified ages might be found to be incapable of consummating the marriage (see p. 50), and whether the unions of children who married *under* the specified ages would be valid depended on whether they remained together: if they parted before the girl had reached her twelfth birthday or the boy his fourteenth, then the marriage was void; if they remained together after the relevant birthday then they were regarded as having ratified the marriage, which would thereafter be regarded as valid.

Q. *Transcribing a marriage register, we discovered an 11-year-old girl marrying a 22-year-old in 1894. The writing is clear, and there's a baptism entry and census data to back it up. Was this legal?*

A. The Registrar General's report for 1894 records only 19 15-year-olds getting married, so 11 really was *exceptionally* young. Even so, it was legally possible. At the time, a marriage under the age of consent (12 for a girl and 14 for a boy) was only voidable, not void. In this case, either party could have challenged the marriage up until her 12th birthday, but as long as they both affirmed it after she reached that age it would be valid. Affirming the marriage did not require a specific declaration; continuing to live together was seen as sufficient. (Many thanks to Helen Barrell and the FreeREG transcribers for sharing this example.)

Somewhat surprisingly, it remained the law until the early twentieth century that girls and boys aged twelve and fourteen respectively could validly marry (apart from a brief period under the Commonwealth when the minimum age was raised to sixteen for boys and fourteen for girls). It was not until the Age of Marriage Act 1929 that the minimum age of marriage was raised to sixteen for both sexes. In contrast to the flexible presumptions of the canon law, this was a strict minimum: for couples marrying after that Act came into force, the marriage would be void if either was found to be below the age of sixteen at the time of the marriage, even if only by one day.

> **Key fact: since May 10th, 1929, the marriage of anyone proven to be below the age of sixteen at the time of the ceremony has been void.**

Sixteen years has remained the minimum age for marriage until today (despite some expressions of unease that it may be too young to make such a decision), the argument being that it would be seen as sanctioning sexual intercourse outside marriage if the minimum age of marriage were higher than the age of consent to sexual intercourse, and because of the pragmatic recognition that raising the age of consent to sexual intercourse would have little if any effect on teenagers' sexual behaviour.

Parental consent and the age of 'free' marriage

In addition to the practical constraints on early marriage (such as amassing the resources to set up a home, and being in an economic position to support a family), there was also the legal requirement that those under a certain age required parental consent in order to marry. Under the canon law the age of 'free' marriage—i.e. the age at which parental consent was no longer necessary—was 21, and this remained the case for first marriages until 1970, the Family Law Reform Act 1969 having reduced the age of majority to 18. Those who remarried after the death of a spouse did not need parental consent to do so, even if they were still under the age of 21; by contrast, those whose first marriage ended in divorce *did* need parental consent to enter into a second marriage if they were still a minor.

So, the law might appear to have been clear when it set out the minimum age at which a person could marry without parental consent, but it is important for the family historian to bear in mind that the legal consequences of failing to secure parental consent, and the issue of whose consent was needed,[1] varied considerably over the period, as we shall see.

i. Until March 24th, 1754

Under the Church's canon law, persons under 21 were directed to obtain parental consent to their marriage. In the case of a marriage by banns, parental consent was to be signified in advance: Canon 62 prescribed that the clergyman was not to marry the couple 'before the Parents or Governours of the Parties to be married, being under the age of twenty and one years, shall either personally, or by sufficient testimony, signify to him their consents given to the said marriage.' If this was not done, an irate parent could forbid the banns. Those who wished to marry by licence were directed by Canon 102 to swear that they were of age or had parental consent, and under Canon 101 were directed to give financial security in support of such statements. In addition, Canon 103 directed that two witnesses swear that parental consent had been obtained.

However, just as with most of the requirements of the canon law (see Chapter Four, p. 75), a lack of parental consent would not invalidate a marriage which had actually taken place. In fact, even *active disapproval* of the marriage of a person under 21 could not invalidate the marriage once the ceremony had taken place, even if the disapproval had been voiced before the ceremony. The reason for this is simple: in the eyes of the Church, a marriage which had been solemnly and duly entered into in the presence of an ordained Anglican clergyman between an unmarried man and an unmarried woman who were of age and not within the prohibited degrees was valid, regardless of objections.

---

1 In addition, if a child was a ward of court, the consent of the Court of Chancery was required for that child's marriage. A marriage celebrated without such consent remained valid, but the parties committed a contempt by so marrying and could be punished.

Key fact: until March 24th, 1754, once the marriage of a minor
had taken place, whether by banns or by licence, it could not
be found to be invalid because of a lack of parental consent, or
even if parental disapproval had been voiced.

For this reason, the question of whose consent was needed attracted
little debate. From the sparse case-law of the time we know that
'parental' consent meant, in the first instance, *paternal* consent. A
mother could also give her consent, but a guardian appointed by a
late father's will enjoyed priority over a mother, and his consent to a
marriage would trump her dissent (and vice versa).

But even though a lack of parental consent did not invalidate a
marriage, the directory requirements of the canon law still exerted
a powerful influence on how couples married. Those who married
under age without securing parental consent risked being censured
by the church courts. Even more significant was the fact that a
clergyman who married a couple without checking that they had the
consent of their parents risked suspension for three years. This inevitably limited the supply of clergymen willing to conduct a marriage
ceremony for underage persons. In London the matter was easy
enough: the parties could repair to the Fleet prison, where clergymen
imprisoned for debt had nothing to lose, and much to gain, from
marrying any couple who presented themselves to be wed. In the
provinces, however, matters were more difficult, and couples might
have to travel some distance to find an obliging clergyman. Family
historians who have been baffled by their ancestors' choice of parish
when marrying might want to look at how popular that particular
parish was, and whether the incumbent regularly married underage
couples (see p. 138).

ii. March 25th, 1754 to August 31st, 1822

Lord Hardwicke's Clandestine Marriages Act 1753 came into force on
March 25th, 1754. Under this, the statute which governed the law of
marriage for almost the next seventy years, it was only possible to
marry either after the calling of banns or by obtaining a licence (see
p. 78). As under the old canon law, once a person had reached the age
of 21 they were free to marry without the need for consent. For those

under 21, either *active parental consent* or a *lack of active dissent* was required, depending on whether the marriage was by licence or by banns. The difference between the two is crucial to understanding when a marriage might be invalidated by a lack of parental consent in this period.

Parental consent to marriages by banns

For individuals below the age of 21 wishing to marry after the calling of banns, active parental consent was not necessary. However, parental *dissent* voiced during the period of the calling of the banns, right up until the ceremony itself, prevented the ceremony from proceeding and so in theory prevented the marriage.

> **Key fact: the parent of a minor could *actively forbid* the banns, and so prevent him or her from marrying.**

If the ceremony did take place in the face of active parental dissent, the dissent was regarded as having invalidated the correct calling of the banns and the marriage would have been void from the start. Since the officiating clergyman was liable to be transported for 14 years, it is perhaps unsurprising that there is no reported example of a court having to decide on the status of such a marriage.

In this context, illegitimate children enjoyed a rare advantage: there was nobody who could legally forbid the banns. But even for legitimate children who had not yet reached the age of majority there would often be no one to forbid the banns: early parental death meant that at least some would be orphaned by the time of their marriage, although the combination of increasing longevity and earlier marriage meant that in the second half of the eighteenth century the majority of parents survived to see (or at least be alive at the time of) the marriages of their children.

Banns and the residency requirements

When it came to a parent's ability to forbid the banns of a minor child, an important factor was that many people under the age of 21 would no longer be living in the parental home. Among the lower orders, children tended to move out at a fairly young age to work as servants or apprentices, long before they married. Class, gender, and economics all determined how long children remained under the parental roof. Lower-class boys were likely to move out far earlier than aristocratic girls, and were thus freer to escape parental control. But the adolescent children of wealthy homes might pay extended visits to friends and relations, giving them opportunities to thwart their parents' wishes. The novels of Jane Austen provide numerous believable examples: Lydia's visit to Brighton facilitates her elopement with Wickham in *Pride & Prejudice*, while in *Emma* Jane Fairfax becomes secretly engaged to Frank Churchill while living with friends. At all levels of society there might be the possibility of validly marrying while away from home, but such possibilities were obviously far more extensive for those who had already established an independent residence away from their parents.

Key fact: a parent might not know that banns had been called for the marriage of a minor child, but their lack of consent did not invalidate the banns.

But even minors living at home might be able to marry in a more distant parish in order to escape parental disapproval. For some couples this might involve an elopement and a temporary residence in the parish where they wished to marry (see p. 62). A marriage could even be had without an actual elopement in towns and cities where there were numerous, closely packed parishes, and where news of the banns being read would not filter back to the parents so easily. Many couples chose to marry surreptitiously in London.

Q. *Late eighteenth-century ancestors of mine married in a parish other than the village where I am sure they were living. I have read elsewhere that this means they were not really married. Is this true?*

A. This is a mistake which is repeated with alarming frequency in guides to family history, and which stems from a failure to appreciate the difference between directory and mandatory requirements. The validity of your ancestors' marriage was not affected by being held in the 'wrong' parish church.

It is most important for family historians to appreciate the implications of the 1753 Act in this regard: the Act required a marriage to take place in the church of a parish where at least one of the parties resided, but this requirement was *directory* rather than *mandatory* (see p. 146), with the result that a marriage that took place in a parish where neither lived was nevertheless still valid.

> **Key fact: because residence requirements have always been directory rather than mandatory, marrying in a parish in which neither party is resident has never had the effect of invalidating the marriage.**

Add to this the fact that active parental consent to the marriage by banns of a person under 21 was not necessary to its validity, and it can be seen that the 1753 Act created a loophole by which minors could evade parental control by calling the banns in a parish where they were unknown and from where word of their proposed marriage was unlikely to get back to their families. Their marriage, once duly entered into, was perfectly valid. Genealogists who find ancestors marrying in parishes to which they seem to have no connection—and this is a very common scenario, even in this period—must not think that such a marriage was void.

The calling of banns in the correct name

The only avenue open to aggrieved parents who learned of their child's marriage too late was to claim that the banns had not been properly called in the first place: for example, if the wrong name had been used. While a marriage could be challenged on this basis whether or not the individual in question was under 21 (see further p. 79), a lack of parental consent and a marriage in a parish to which neither belonged might well convince the court that the wrong name had been used deliberately and lead to the marriage being declared void.

Q. *I have discovered that in 1800 my ancestors married in a parish to which neither belonged. Both were clearly underage, and both omitted the middle names with which they had been baptised. Was this void?*

A. Had this marriage been challenged at the time by the parent of either spouse, a court might well have declared it to be void, if it felt that the names had been omitted to disguise the fact that this particular boy and girl were getting married (for example, if they were usually known by their middle names). But there were only a handful of cases in which irate parents succeeded in setting aside the marriages of their minor children on the basis that the banns had not been properly called. As Chapter Four has shown, the courts were much less willing to annul a marriage on the basis of the wrong name being used if some time had passed since the wedding, and a marriage not found to be void must now be presumed to have been valid.

Parental consent to marriages by licence

By contrast, prior parental consent *was* required to the marriage by licence of a person under the age of 21. The 1753 Act explicitly specified that such a marriage without parental consent was void. This new rule meant that it was also necessary to set out clearly whose consent was required, and the Act accordingly laid down a strict hierarchy. Heading the list was the father; if he had died then it was the responsibility of any guardian appointed by the father's will; if none had been appointed then the mother was entitled to give her consent (unless she had remarried, in which case she lost this right); and in the absence of any of the above persons the consent of a guardian appointed by the Court of Chancery was needed. (It should be remembered that the parents of an *illegitimate* child had no power either to allow or forbid their child's marriage by licence. Illegitimate children under 21 did of course have the option of marrying by banns.)

So it was not merely that a lack of any parental consent would render the marriage void; it was also the case that a lack of the *correct* person's consent would render the marriage void. In the apparently harsh 1819 case of *Hayes v Watts*, the bride's mother had given consent to the marriage going ahead, the father having emigrated to America some years previously and not having been heard of since. When the father returned to England, alive and well, his daughter's marriage was annulled after it had lasted for eighteen years. (Intriguingly, it was the daughter herself who had sought the annulment, raising the suspicion that the lack of fatherly consent was being used as a reason for getting out of the marriage!)

But the case of *Hayes v Watts*, in which the courts could find no way of upholding the marriage within the terms of the 1753 Act, was highly exceptional. In actual fact, the courts turned out to be most unhappy at the idea of invalidating a marriage of any reasonable duration purely on the technicality that parental consent had not been given beforehand. Even without active parental consent prior to the marriage by licence of a person under 21, the courts were willing to *infer* the existence of prior parental consent to the marriage from subsequent parental acquiescence in the marriage or even from a lack of active parental disapproval before the marriage took place. By way of example, in one 1811 case (*Smith v Huson*) the court inferred from the fact that the bride's father had not actively forbidden the marriage to conclude that he must have implicitly given his consent, and therefore upheld the marriage. In a case heard in 1808 (*Osborn v Goldham*), it was perfectly obvious that the mother had not given her prior consent, as she was only told about the wedding after it had taken place. Once again, though, the court upheld the marriage on the basis of the mother's subsequent acquiescence, simply because she had not expressed active disapproval.

Key fact: though the letter of the law required parental consent to a marriage by licence of a person under 21, the courts were reluctant to invalidate marriages which lacked consent if this was subsequently alleged by either husband or wife.

So a marriage which apparently contravened the letter of the law could nevertheless be held to be valid.

Q. *I have discovered the marriage licence of an ancestor who I know from the baptism register to have been just under 21 when she married in 1760, but the licence states that she is 'of age'. Was the marriage valid?*

A. Given the way that the courts bent over backwards to uphold marriages which had actually taken place, at least if any period of time had elapsed since the wedding, there is a strong possibility that in a case of this kind the court would simply decide that the evidence of age was inconclusive and that the bride was in fact 21 when she married. A baptism, after all, might occur weeks or even months after the birth of a child. In one case the court even rejected the evidence of the family bible and the bride's own father on the basis that a mistake might have been made. In other words, if there was evidence that parental consent had not been given, the courts insisted on very clear proof of the spouse's age.

Q. *I have uncovered the marriage of an ancestor who was clearly under 21 when she married by licence in 1772, but I have not found any evidence of parental consent. Does this mean that the marriage was void and their children illegitimate?*

A. No. Firstly, the lack of evidence of consent does not mean that consent was not given. Secondly, even if consent was not given, or there was active disapproval, proving this was difficult enough even during the parties' lifetimes and almost impossible after their deaths. Legally, a marriage that has not been declared void by a court must be assumed to be valid. Given that only a very small number of cases even came to court, and still fewer resulted in the marriage being annulled (see below), it is therefore extremely unlikely that any given marriage involving a minor was ever declared invalid.

Key fact: even if an ancestor demonstrably married below the age of majority, this does not mean that their marriage was invalid. Unless a court declared the marriage void, it must be presumed to have been valid.

Finally, it is worth noting that under the 1753 Act a minor was entitled to apply to the Lord Chancellor to give his consent to the marriage if a mother or guardian was unreasonably withholding consent (although a father's refusal of consent could not be overridden in this way).

Despite fears that the codification of the canon law into the Marriage Act 1753 would lead to numerous marriages being invalidated, very few actually came before the courts before 1800, with only six reaching the Court of Arches, the appeal court for the province of Canterbury. Only in the first decade of the nineteenth century did the number of challenges begin to rise. What concerned the courts was not so much those cases in which an aggrieved parent sought to annul the marriage of an underage child, but rather those cases in which a husband or wife sought to argue that their *own* longstanding marriage was invalid because one of them had not had parental consent. While the number remained small (between 1800 and 1810 the Court of Arches heard a total of eight cases alleging that a minor had married by licence without parental consent, rising to 17 between 1811 and 1820) this use of annulment as a substitute for divorce was sufficiently worrying to galvanise Parliament into action. But speed is not always conducive to workable legislation, and no fewer than three pieces of marriage legislation were passed between 1822 and 1823. As a result, family historians looking at marriages in the early nineteenth century must pay close attention to dates in order to determine which set of rules would have applied.

iii. September 1st, 1822 to March 25th, 1823

The Marriage Act 1822 made it harder to get married in the first place (by introducing the need for sworn affidavits confirming parental consent and residence—see p. 85) but removed the sanction that a failure to comply would render the marriage void. It also attempted to stop individuals relying on the fact that they or their spouse had been underage at the time of the marriage by retrospectively validating all marriages of minors by licence where parental consent had not been given but where the parties had continued to live together until death or the passage of the new Act.

> Key fact: marriages by licence of persons under 21 entered into on or before July 22nd, 1822 without the correct parental consent automatically became valid after that date.

Past marriages by banns, by contrast, were not affected by the Act.

iv. March 26th, 1823 to October 31st, 1823

The 1822 Act proved unworkable, and was swiftly repealed by a further Act. Between March 26th and October 31st, 1823, marriages were once again conducted in accordance with the provisions of the 1753 Act (with the important proviso that marriages celebrated by licence should not be deemed invalid on the basis of lack of parental consent). This, however, was merely a holding measure while a more satisfactory compromise was found.

v. November 1st, 1823 to June 30th, 1837

The Marriage Act 1823 subsequently established the basic rule (which still applies today) that a marriage will only be void if the couple *knowingly and wilfully* fail to comply with certain specified requirements. As a result, if a marriage involving one or more persons under 21 was celebrated after banns had been called, it could still be found to be void if the parties had had the banns called in the wrong names in an attempt to avoid knowledge of the intended marriage reaching their parents.

By contrast, a lack of parental consent ceased to be a ground for invalidating a marriage by licence, even if the couple had knowingly and wilfully married without consent. By way of deterrence, however, it was provided that minors who obtained a licence by false oaths (for example by swearing that they were of age or had parental consent) might forfeit any property that would otherwise accrue to them by virtue of the marriage.

vi. July 1st, 1837 to December 31st, 1949

When new options for marriage were introduced by the Marriage Act 1836 (see Chapter Four), the rules on parental consent were extended to these new situations. So, if a couple married in a civil ceremony, consent was required of any person whose consent would have been required if the marriage had been by licence. As had been the case before July 1st, 1837, the lack of positive parental consent did not invalidate the marriage, but a minor making a false statement risked forfeiting any property that would have accrued to them as a result of the marriage. However, as with the calling of the banns, a parent was able to forbid the grant of a superintendent registrar's certificate and thereby prevent the marriage from going ahead. If the marriage did go ahead despite this, it would be void.

Key fact: after July 1st, 1837, a marriage may still be void if it takes place after the person whose consent is required has forbidden the banns or the grant of a certificate.

Between 1837 and 1949, changes were also made to *whose* consent was necessary to the marriage of a minor. The role of the paterfamilias was no longer unchallenged, and mothers were increasingly acquiring legal rights within the family sphere. As a result, in 1925 the Guardianship of Infants Act included a complex provision identifying whose consent to a marriage was necessary in different circumstances: if the parents of a legitimate child were living together, *both* had to consent; if they had divorced or separated, the consent of the person to whom custody had been committed was necessary; if one had deserted the other, the consent of the deserted parent alone was required; if both parents had been deprived of custody, then the law required the consent of the person to whose custody the child had been committed; and if the child had been born outside marriage, the consent of the mother alone was required.

Given the fact that the consent of *two* people might now be required, rather than just one, there was also a need to simplify and modernise the circumstances in which it was possible to dispense with consent. So it was provided that the necessity of a certain person's consent could be dispensed with if it could not be obtained by reason of their absence, inaccessibility or disability. If this person was the only person whose consent was necessary, the Registrar General might dispense with the requirement of consent; alternatively, a court could grant consent. If there was another person whose consent was required, a superintendent registrar might dispense with the consent of the person who was unavailable to give consent. It is nevertheless likely that there were more couples who married underage by falsely claiming to have parental consent than there were couples who took the route of applying to a court.

vii. January 1st, 1950 to the present day

The Marriage Act 1949 abolished the rules which had existed since 1823 relating to the forfeiture of property if a minor married after swearing false oaths. In other respects it simply consolidated the existing requirements relating to parental consent, providing that it would not be necessary to prove that parental consent had been given to the marriage of a minor, and that no evidence may be given to prove the contrary 'in any proceedings touching the validity of the marriage.' Like much of the law of marriage, therefore, the significance of the need for parental consent today lies in its preventative role, rather than in its effect on marriages that have actually taken place.

Q. *I recently discovered that my late mother, who was 17 when she married by banns in 1952, did not have parental consent. Am I illegitimate?*

A. A lack of active parental consent to your mother's marriage could not invalidate it, but if the banns were actively *forbidden* by her parents this would have invalidated the marriage. If however the marriage was never challenged in court during the lifetimes of the parties then it is unlikely that a court would now overturn its validity, even assuming that an 'interested third party' with the legal status to launch a challenge were to make themselves known.

THE TIMING OF THE MARRIAGE

A further question of particular interest to the family historian is at what stage in a couple's relationship their marriage took place. How old were couples when they married? Had they lived together before the wedding? And were they waiting for evidence of fertility before embarking on marriage?

At what age did couples marry?

For the genealogist trying to decide on the likelihood of a particular marriage being that of their ancestor, it is useful to bear in mind that, contrary to popular assumptions, child marriages were rare

	1600-49	1650-99	1700-49	1750-99	1800-49
Grooms	28.0	27.8	27.5	26.4	25.3
Brides	26.0	26.5	26.2	24.9	23.4

Table 5.1 Mean age at first marriage, 1600-1850 (Wrigley & Schofield, *The Population History of England 1541-1871* (CUP, 1989), p. 255, table 7.26)

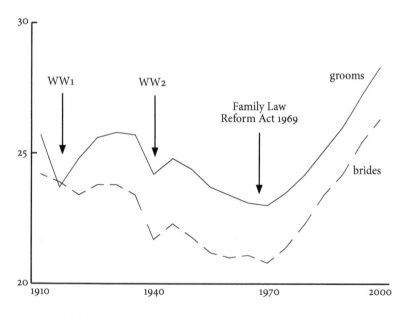

Fig. 5.1 Mean age at first marriage, 1910-2000
(source: Schoen & Canudas-Romo (2005) 51 *Population Studies* 135)

throughout the period covered by this book. You should accordingly be wary of assuming that a potential match where the bride was only 12 years old is automatically the correct one: this was possible, but certainly not typical. Throughout the seventeenth, eighteenth and nineteenth centuries couples generally did not embark on marriage until their mid twenties (see Table 5.1, p. 124). While official statistics on age at marriage were not collected until the nineteenth century, parish studies provide estimates that can be used as a general guide.

From the 1830s onwards, data was collected more systematically. The marriage register contained a column for brides and grooms to state their age, although not all did so and some merely recorded 'of full age'. Even at the end of the nineteenth century, more than 10% of spinsters and bachelors did not give their age when they married, and for widows and widowers this rose to around 40%. Of those marrying for the first time between 1850 and 1899, the average age was a little under 26 for men and a little over 24 for women. The percentage of grooms marrying under the age of 21 remained relatively low, rising from just 5% in 1850 to 8.4% in 1876 and back again to 5% by 1899, while the percentage of underage brides was a little higher but followed a similar trajectory (15% in 1850, 22.7% in 1876, and 16.5% by 1899).

These are, of course, only averages. Age at marriage not only varied over time but also according to class, location and occupation. And while very few married under the age of 16, there were always those who married for the first time in their 40s and 50s. (The Registrar General's report for 1870 even noted the marriage of a pair who were both in their 80s.)

Once we reach the twentieth century, improved recording means that the data is more reliable. As Fig. 5.1 (p. 124) shows, the average age of marriage plunged to a historic low in the mid-twentieth century, but then climbed again, reaching the levels of the early 1600s by the year 2000. Since then it has risen still further: by 2010 the average age of brides marrying for the first time was over 30.

Today, however, it is not the need to amass resources in order to set up a home that leads to marriage being deferred, but rather that couples are choosing to live together in advance of the wedding. The

Case-Study: Investigating Addresses at Marriage in Bethnal Green

One way of testing whether couples were living where they claimed to be living when they married is to look for them in the census. Ninety-nine couples married in the Bethnal Green churches of St John, St Jude and St Matthew in the three months following the 1891 Census. Of these, 42 gave the *same* address in the marriage register, but on investigation only eight of these 42 were actually living at the same address. Of the 57 who gave *different* addresses, three in fact turned out to be living at the *same* address, giving a total of eleven couples living at the same address. The number of couples actually living at the same address was therefore around a quarter of what one would have concluded by relying solely on the addresses recorded on the marriage certificates.

But even the eleven couples who were living at the same address were not necessarily 'cohabiting', in the modern sense. In five cases, the address was occupied by either the bride or groom's parents and siblings, with the future spouse being described as a visitor or lodger. In a further five cases, the pair had passed themselves off as 'married' in the census and the relationship seems to have been of some duration. The final case was particularly intriguing, since it involved a man who was recorded twice in the census: once as residing with his parents and siblings, and once as living with the woman he married a week later!

An obvious explanation would be that those who gave the *same* address while in fact living at *different* addresses were referring to their future matrimonial home, but this seems not to have been the case. The more likely (and unexpected) answer is that there was a financial advantage to passing oneself off as cohabiting unmarried: the Victorian authorities were so concerned that couples might be living together outside marriage that some clergymen and civil registrars offered to marry cohabiting couples for free. This could explain why couples who were *not* in fact living together might represent themselves as cohabiting.

vast majority of twenty-first century marriages are preceded by a period of cohabitation, sometimes extremely lengthy. But was this the case for our ancestors?

Did couples live together before marrying?

Here it is useful to work backwards from the systematic collection of data in the twentieth century to the evidence that can be used for the nineteenth century. It was only in the 1980s that pre-marital cohabitation became established as the norm. By the end of that decade couples were more likely than not to live together before marrying; in the late 1970s, however, fewer than one-fifth of couples marrying for the first time had shared a home before marriage. Data for previous decades comes from retrospective surveys (in which people were asked to recall their behaviour earlier in their lives), and suggests that the proportion of couples cohabiting before marriage before the 1970s was even lower, perhaps as low as 1% for those marrying in the 1950s.

This might surprise those family historians who possess a marriage certificate for their Victorian ancestors apparently recording that they were living at the same address at the date of the wedding. Any perusal of a marriage register will show that it was not uncommon for couples to give the same address—particularly, but not exclusively, in large cities. Taking this information at face value, one might jump to the conclusion that Victorian England had relatively high levels of pre-marital cohabitation, as high indeed as in the 1980s. Further investigation, however, indicates that addresses given in the marriage certificate simply cannot be relied upon, either as an indication of pre-marital cohabitation or even as evidence of actual residence, as the case-study of Bethnal Green shows (p. 126).

Key fact: addresses recorded on marriage certificates cannot be relied upon as evidence of pre-marital cohabitation.

Nor was it only in big cities that one finds such patterns. A study of a very different population—a sample taken from those marrying in a range of parishes across rural Dorset in 1891—found similar results. Of the 70 couples in the sample, 28 (40%) were claiming to be living at the same address when they married, but on investigating the census returns this proved true of only seven (10%), and only four of them were passing themselves off as husband and wife. Of the 42 who claimed to be living at a different address, only one couple turned out to be living at the same address.

Were couples waiting for proof of fertility before marrying?

Working out just how many brides were pregnant on their wedding day is no easy task. Some cases are clear-cut, for example where the birth of a child occurred within days or weeks of the wedding; more difficult are those cases where the interval between marriage and a first child is eight to ten months. How many of the births that occurred *under* nine months after the wedding can be explained by premature birth (more common if the mother is engaged in physical labour, is undernourished, or is seriously underweight) rather than premarital sex? How many baptisms that occurred *more* than nine months after the wedding conceal a pre-marital conception because of the time lapse between birth and baptism? How many first children were conceived before marriage but died unbaptized? And how many women lost a pre-marital pregnancy to a miscarriage, leaving only a subsequent post-marital conception to be recorded?

Much more research is needed before we can answer these questions with certainty, but an exploratory study suggests that some of the claims that have been made about the extent of bridal pregnancy may need to be revisited. Of the 832 couples who married across Northamptonshire in 1745, a subsequent baptism has been traced for 424. Fig. 5.2 (p. 129) shows the interval between the wedding and the baptism.

Intriguingly, in all of the cases where a couple had borne a child before their marriage, and in most of the cases where the baptism was recorded within two months of the marriage, the couple had married in the parish where they were resident. In such cases, one can infer that it was important for them to show the community that they were truly married, or perhaps that this was a wedding instigated by the parish, if one party had proved reluctant. There are also a handful of cases where the child was brought to be baptised within three to four months of the wedding, and it would appear that these couples had

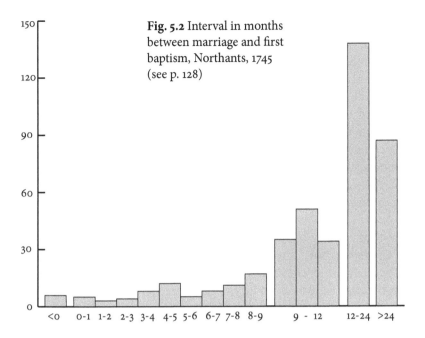

Fig. 5.2 Interval in months between marriage and first baptism, Northants, 1745 (see p. 128)

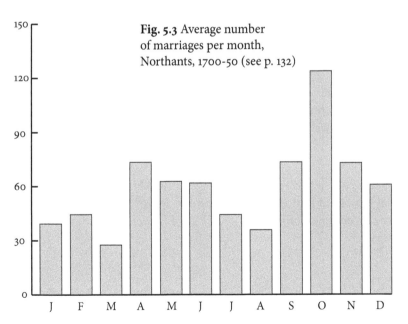

Fig. 5.3 Average number of marriages per month, Northants, 1700-50 (see p. 132)

married in a parish to which neither belonged in order to conceal the fact that the bride was heavily pregnant.

Overall, however, the most striking finding from Northamptonshire is that the majority of births occurred more than a year after the wedding. This evidence is more consistent with couples delaying a sexual relationship until after the wedding than it is with the commonly-held belief that it was necessary to wait for evidence of fertility before embarking on marriage. The family historian who has found a baptism record for a couple's first child and is looking for the marriage can generally expect to find it between ten months and two years earlier.

For those tracing marriages before the mid-eighteenth century there is a potential trap of which they need to be aware. Until September of 1752, England and Wales used the Julian calendar, and the New Year started on March 25th. The day after December 31st, 1750, for example, was January 1st, *1750*. This can make quite a difference to our interpretation of the sequence of events:

Q: *I have found a record of my ancestor being baptised on March 1st, 1700, and his parents getting married on April 1st, 1700. Was the child illegitimate?*

A: No. What is recorded as 'March 1st, 1700' is what we would now call March 1st, *1701*. He was in fact baptised 11 months *after* his parents' wedding.

Choosing a date

Once a couple had reached the stage of deciding to marry, how did they go about choosing a date for the wedding, and what factors influenced their choice?

Seasons

The Church's prohibited seasons

The Church of England retained the Catholic Church's pre-Reformation prohibitions on marrying at certain particularly holy times of year (for example Lent), and at the start of our period in 1600 the church calendar, with its prohibited seasons, still exerted some influence over when couples married.

Marriages were *allowed* from January 13th (the day before the Feast of St Hilary) until Septuagesima Sunday (the third Sunday before Lent). They were then *prohibited* all the way through Lent until eight days after Easter (the day after Low Sunday). From then they were *allowed* again, for a relatively short period, until Rogation Sunday (the fifth Sunday after Easter). Then they were *prohibited* again until Trinity Sunday (the first Sunday after Pentecost). From then, they were *allowed* all the way through until the start of Advent (the fourth Sunday before Christmas Day).

But the Church had also retained the practice of selling licences to circumvent its own prohibitions (though this was criticised by Puritan reformers), so that marriages by licence could in fact be celebrated during prohibited seasons. While a clergyman might be admonished for celebrating a marriage after banns during a prohibited season, the marriage itself would not be vulnerable to challenge on this basis.

Key fact: marriages solemnized during the Church's prohibited seasons were nevertheless valid.

The fact that the prohibitions were not universally observed can be a positive advantage for the genealogist, since the timing of a marriage might give some clue to an ancestor's religious scruples. There is unfortunately no easy answer to when marriages were prohibited, since it varied with the timing of Easter, but the determined family historian can find historical calendars with moveable feasts online, once they are sure of the year in which an ancestor married.

In 1644 the short-lived *Directory of Public Worship* tried to sweep away the prohibited seasons, which were perceived as 'popish', stating that marriages could take place 'at any time of year'. The *Directory* did, however, continue to see certain days as unsuitable for marriage (see below, p. 133). Come the Restoration of the English monarchy in 1660 the church's prohibited seasons were revived, although in this as in other aspects the Church experienced difficulties in imposing its authority.

The agricultural calendar

In the eighteenth century the timing of marriage was more influenced by the agricultural calendar, than by that of the Church. The busy summer months had fewer marriages than the quieter autumn period, as Fig. 5.3 (p. 129), showing marriages across Northamptonshire in the first half of the eighteenth century, illustrates. By this time the idea of there being prohibited seasons had clearly lost most of the hold it had once had: Christmas marriages were popular, although Lent remained a relatively unusual time to marry.

Urbanization

In the nineteenth century, the move to less seasonally dependent occupations saw a flattening out of marriages across the year. Much, of course, depended on location: in rural Northamptonshire, July remained the least and October the most popular month to marry, while August saw fewer marriages than February. At Manchester Cathedral, by contrast, April and August were the most popular months, although the single most popular day was the last Sunday before Lent, indicating that old ideas still held some sway even among urbanites.

Tax, and the hope of good weather

The mid-twentieth century saw March weddings becoming briefly popular for tax reasons, since men who married before the end of the tax year were entitled to the married man's allowance for the entire preceding year. This ended abruptly in 1969, when the rules were changed so that those marrying in March received only one month's worth of the year's allowance. Today, an increased focus on marriage as an event means that the summer wedding has become the most popular. According to the latest figures, almost six times as many people choose to marry in August as compared to January.

Days

Sundays

Before 1754, when marriage was regulated by the Church, the canon law stated that marriages should be celebrated during divine service,

132

i.e. on Sundays or holy days, and an analysis of the weekly distribution of marriages does indeed show that Sundays were popular, particularly for those marrying by banns. Of course, the celebrations associated with weddings were problematic for those of a more puritanical inclination, who wished Sundays to be devoted to prayer, and in 1644 the *Directory of Public Worship* advised that marriages should not be solemnized 'on the Lord's day' (although without going so far as to say that such marriages would not be valid).

Key fact: although the law has at various times directed that marriages should or should not be solemnized on certain days of the week, marriages which failed to observe this rule have nevertheless always been valid.

Sundays continued to be favoured throughout the nineteenth century, particularly in urban areas. This was, after all, the one full day of leisure for working men and women: in 1864, over 46% of marriages in working-class East London took place on a Sunday, as compared to a national average of 32%. Today, Sunday only remains a popular day to marry for non-Christian religious communities.

Mondays

Perhaps more surprising is the popularity of Monday as a day to marry. In 1864 it was second only to Sunday in England and Wales as a whole, and in a survey of marriages across Northamptonshire in 1836, Monday emerged as the clear favourite. This may suggest that rural areas were slower to adopt a standard working week, and that the old idea of 'Saint Monday'—being a day when the week's work had not really begun in earnest—still held some sway.

Saturdays

In the last decades of the nineteenth century, Saturdays began to increase in popularity as the practice emerged of giving workers a half-day off. This was particularly marked in industrial cities such as Manchester, where between 1864 and 1881 the percentage of marriages held on a Sunday more than halved (from over 34% to under 17%), and Saturday became the most popular day of the week to marry.

Hours

Since marriages were a matter of public interest, they were supposed to take place at a time when they would be visible to the outside world. The canons of 1604 stated that marriages should take place between 8 a.m. and noon. Weddings that took place outside these hours were technically clandestine (see p. 17) but still valid. The Marriage Act 1753 made no mention of the hours within which marriage should be celebrated, but the Marriage Act 1823 provided that clergymen who knowingly and wilfully solemnized a marriage before 8 a.m. or after midday would be guilty of a felony and liable for transportation for 14 years, unless they were acting on the authority of a special licence. Not until the Marriage Act 1886 were the permitted hours for marriage extended, and then only to 3 p.m. The motivation for the change was to make it easier for registrars to fulfil their role of attending dissenting marriages, but the new rules were also thought more suitable to both the working hours of the lower classes and the changing social habits of the upper classes. The idea that marriage should take place within the hours of daylight still prevailed, however, with the Secretary of State opposing the initial proposal of allowing marriages to take place up to 4 p.m. on the basis that by that time it would be dark in winter. When in 1934 it was proposed that the hours within which marriages could be celebrated should be extended to 6 p.m., it seems to have been the widespread availability of electric lighting which made the old restrictions redundant. Any suspicion that the change was to meet the wishes of the smarter set, who might want to follow the wedding with a cocktail party, was firmly rebuffed in the House of Lords: it was, said one peer, rather to meet the wishes of those working men and women who could not spare the time, or rather the loss of pay, to celebrate their marriage during the middle of the day.

From October 1st, 2012, all statutory restrictions on the timing of marriages were removed. The Church of England, however, continues to require marriages to be solemnised between 8 a.m. and 6 p.m.

Key fact: canon law and statute law have for centuries set out the hours within which couples are expected to marry, but these rules have always been directory rather than mandatory and so a failure to observe them has never rendered the marriage invalid.

FURTHER READING

On age at marriage
Rogers, N. 'Money, Marriage, Mobility: The Big Bourgeoisie of Hanoverian London' (1999) 24 *Journal of Family History* 19

Wrigley and Schofield, *The Population History of England, 1541-1871* (Cambridge University Press, 1981)

Wall, R. 'Marriage, Residence, and Occupational Choices of Senior and Junior Siblings in the English Past' (1996) 1 *The History of the Family* 259

Wilcox, P. 'Marriage, Mobility and Domestic Service in Victorian Cambridge' (1982) 29 *Local Population Studies* 19.

On parental consent to marriage
Probert, R. 'Control over Marriage in England and Wales, 1753-1823: The Clandestine Marriages Act of 1753 in Context' (2009) 27 *Law and History Review* 413-450

On pre-marital cohabitation
Probert, R. *The Legal Regulation of Cohabitation, 1600-2010: From Fornicators to Family* (Cambridge University Press, 2012)

On choosing a date
Boulton, J. 'Economy of Time? Wedding Days and the Working Week in the Past' (1989) 43 *Local Population Studies* 28

Cressy, D. *Birth, Marriage and Death: Ritual, Religion and the Life-Cycle in Tudor and Stuart England* (Oxford University Press, 1997)

WHERE

FROM 1600 TO MARCH 24TH, 1754
FROM MARCH 25TH, 1754 TO JUNE 30TH, 1837
FROM JULY 1ST, 1837
MARRIAGE ACROSS THE GLOBE

One of the most important practical questions for the family historian is where their ancestors might have married, since this will obviously lead them to where the record of the marriage is likely to be found. For the majority of our period, the law has tried to channel couples into marrying in the place where they are known and resident. But it has not always succeeded. And in truth it did not try too hard to enforce the requirement of marrying in one's parish of residence, since a failure to do so has never rendered the marriage void.

Key fact: English law has always taken a pragmatic approach to a couple's choice of parish. A failure to marry in one's parish of residence has by itself never had an adverse effect on a marriage's validity.

For the family historian investigating speculative matches, it is useful to know just how likely it was that a bride and groom might have married in a parish to which they did not belong, and to gain an idea of the range of distances they might be expected to have travelled. This chapter draws on data from over 5,000 marriages across England and Wales in order to give a better idea of where a couple might have married relative to their later place of abode.

Discovering where a couple married can also open up a whole range of further fascinating questions. If they married in a parish to which they seem to have no connection, what reasons did they have for doing so? Was the bride pregnant, or did their parents disapprove of the match? Or was there some more prosaic reason for the choice? If you have discovered that your ancestors married in a different jurisdiction altogether (see p. 153), other interesting questions emerge: would English law automatically recognize that marriage as valid, and, if not, what factors might determine whether it was recognized or not?

From 1600 to March 24th, 1754

The canon law specified that marriages should be celebrated in the parish where at least one of the parties was resident. However, as with most of the requirements of the canon law, this was directory rather than mandatory, and a marriage would be valid even if it was celebrated in a parish to which the couple had no link whatsoever.

How many couples married in a parish to which neither belonged? As Fig. 6.1 (p. 138) shows, prior to 1754 quite a high proportion of marriages were celebrated outside the parish where the bride and groom were resident (and the relatively poor quality of record-keeping means that in a large number of cases their parish of residence was not stated in the marriage register).

Other evidence suggests that a high proportion of those marriages in Fig. 6.1 for which no parish was recorded were in fact perfectly regular. In 225 of the marriages celebrated across Northamptonshire in 1745, it was impossible to tell from the marriage register whether or not one or both of the parties were from the parish where the wedding took place, but further investigation established that in 90 cases either the bride or the groom had been baptized in that parish (and in a further 35 cases the couple went on to have children in that parish). This pattern is very different from that for couples marrying in a parish to which neither belonged, and suggests that in many cases the origin of the bride and groom was not recorded simply because they were known locally and there was no need to do so.

Of those who we know married in the parish to which at least one belonged, in most cases (around two-thirds of the total) *both* parties were from that parish. If only one of them was from the parish where they married, it was more likely to be the bride than the groom: in

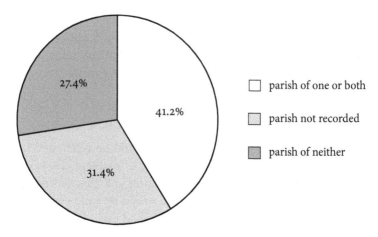

Fig. 6.1 Where Northamptonshire couples married, 1700-1751 (see p. 137)

the Northamptonshire sample, three times as many couples married in the bride's parish as opposed to the groom's parish.

Reasons for marrying in a different parish

Any marriage celebrated in a parish to which neither party belonged was technically 'clandestine'. i.e., not in accordance with all the requirements of the canon law. But the genealogist should not infer underhand motives for such a marriage:

Q. *I have discovered that in 1730 my ancestors married in a parish ten miles from the parish where they were born and where their children were later baptized. Was this an elopement? Can we assume that the bride and groom were marrying in defiance of parental wishes?*

A. Not necessarily. There could be a number of reasons for this choice of parish. You ought to consider whether the church in which they married was particularly popular, whether the incumbent was shared with another parish or was only a temporary appointment, whether the church was open for use at the time, and whether there was a family connection to the parish.

Convenience, cost, privacy

Before 1754, one finds considerable local variation, with some parishes seeing a volume of marriages grossly disproportionate to their size, and others hardly any. In some cases this was no doubt because the clergyman there did not ask too many questions, or perhaps charged a lower fee than others. Another reason for the popularity of otherwise obscure parishes might be that the incumbent had the right to grant licences, enabling couples to marry with a greater degree of privacy and speed.

The lack of other options

Sometimes the couples marrying in a particular parish did so because of the lack of other options. In the first half of the eighteenth century quite a few couples travelled from the Northamptonshire village of Kilsby to be married in either Lilbourne or Brockhall, both popular places for marriage. At the time, however, it seems that Kilsby did not have a permanent incumbent, so Kilsby couples did not have the choice of marrying there. You might want to look at the baptism, marriage and burial registers from the time of the marriage to see who was responsible for conducting such rites. If you find a quick turnover of names, this might suggest that the parish did not have a permanent incumbent, and would explain why a couple who were born and had their children baptized in one parish nevertheless chose to marry in another.

Alternatively, the church might simply have been undergoing repairs or been temporarily out of use. This is the reason behind the popularity of certain London churches in the latter part of the seventeenth century, after the Great Fire swept through the city and destroyed 87 of the 109 churches located there. While temporary places of worship were made available during the process of rebuilding, these seem not to have been particularly attractive (one was unflatteringly described as a 'shed') and it was unsurprising that couples preferred to be married in other, surviving churches.

Case-Study: Bridal Family Links
to the Parish of Marriage

Across Northamptonshire, 230 of the 832 couples who married in 1745 did so in a parish to which they apparently did not belong. Such marriages, if this was indeed the case, were technically 'clandestine' for this reason alone, even if they complied with the canon law in all other respects (see definition, p. 17). Since such marriages accounted for over one-quarter of the marriages that took place across Northamptonshire that year, this would at first sight seem to suggest a widespread disregard of the canon law. However, on further investigation links between the parish of marriage and the bride's family began to emerge.

In 102 cases (just over 44% of the total) there seemed to be some connection between the bride's family and the parish where the marriage took place.

In 58 cases (a quarter of the total), other women sharing the bride's maiden name had married in that parish in the previous decades. For example, when Ann Jenoway of Cold Ashby married in Ravensthorpe in 1745, she was following in the footsteps of Lettice, Elizabeth, and Mary Jenoway, who had married there in 1700, 1703 and 1704 respectively. With more common surnames, of course, matching names are not necessarily irrefutable evidence of a family link. It was however interesting that there were no such matches for the Joneses and Wilsons in the sample, suggesting that the matches found were not mere coincidence.

In a further 44 cases (just under one fifth of the total) men sharing the bride's maiden name had married in that same parish. For example, Thomas Naseby of Kilsby married in Brockhall in 1724; 21 years later Elizabeth Naseby of Kilsby also married in Brockhall. Perhaps both had good reasons for marrying in a parish that attracted a disproportionate number of extraparochial brides and grooms, or perhaps Elizabeth was simply marrying in Brockhall because that was where her relative Thomas had married a generation earlier.

A link between the parishes

Another possibility is that there was some link between the parish where the marriage took place and where the couple are thought to have lived. Again, Kilsby provides an example of the reasons that might link two parishes. For a short period in the 1730s, Kilsby couples regularly travelled to Long Buckby, around seven miles away. This seems baffling, until it is realised that the two parishes shared a vicar. Resident in Long Buckby, he seems to have preferred Kilsby couples to come to him rather than travelling to Kilsby! A quick comparison of whose signature appears in the relevant records can highlight whether this might be the explanation.

A link between the family and the other parish

A further possibility, and one particularly worth exploring, is that the couple *did* have some connection with the parish where they married. When looking at several hundred Northamptonshire marriages that seem to have taken place in the wrong parish (see the case-study on p. 140), it was intriguing how often some link emerged—be it the parents of either spouse having married in that parish, the bride having been baptized there, or other family members clearly being resident there. A family tradition of marrying in a particular parish may also explain the choice of parish in a number of cases.

So a marriage that seems out of place may in fact lead you to new information about your ancestors. Of course, the possibility of a defiant elopement can never be ruled out, but it is far less likely than more innocent explanations.

The reverse is also true: a bride or groom might be described as being 'of this parish' when their connection with that parish was relatively short-term. Very short-term residents might be noted as 'sojourners', but those who had been living in a parish for a year or so, perhaps on account of their employment, might well have no reason to marry in that parish if their family lived elsewhere. To take Kilsby as an example again, it is significant that the majority of those who married outside the village, in a parish to which neither on the face of it belonged, did not have their children baptized in Kilsby either. Indeed, some had no discernable link with Kilsby other than being described as being 'of Kilsby' in the marriage register of the parish where they wed. Such nuggets of evidence as to residence can turn out to be false trails.

How far afield might couples marry?

So where should genealogists be looking for ancestors' marriages in this period? A number of studies that I have carried out cast light on how far afield one may need to look for a marriage. Five different cohorts were examined: (i) people bringing children to be baptized in the twenty years before the 1753 Act came into force in the parishes of Kilsby, St Mary on the Scilly Isles, and York's Holy Trinity, Goodramgate; (ii) people examined as to their settlement in the Wiltshire parish of Bradford-on-Avon in the first half of the eighteenth century; and (iii) people listed in a 1782 'census' of Cardington in Bedfordshire who had married before 1754.

As Fig. 6.2 (p. 144) shows, much depended on the type of parish. The biggest contrast is between St Mary (Scilly Isles) and Holy Trinity (York), for the obvious reason that in an urban parish it is very easy to move between parishes, while on an island the options are somewhat more limited. Generally, however, as the results from Cardington and Bradford-on-Avon illustrate, one can expect to find that around 40 per cent of those baptizing children in a particular parish also married there. Kilsby, with only 24 per cent, was particularly low for the reasons discussed above.

The studies of Cardington and Bradford-on-Avon are also very good illustrations of how far the likelihood of tracing a marriage depends on the information available to the family historian. Cardington, for example, is located in the middle of Bedfordshire, which has one of the best collections of surviving registers of any county in England, and the chances of tracing a marriage that took place elsewhere in Bedfordshire are extremely high. This is not the case for Bradford-on-Avon, as many of the parishes where couples claimed to have married have gaps in their marriage registers at the crucial period.

Two clear trends emerge from the settlement examinations in Bradford-on-Avon (Table 6.1, p. 143): first, that the percentage of marriages traced increases with the information provided, especially information relating to the location of the marriage; secondly, that the percentage traced rises dramatically in the wake of the 1753 Act across all categories. (The results would have been higher still had it not been for the presence of six soldiers, accompanied by wives for whom only first names were recorded and who came from distant parts of the country.)

	Number of marriages traced (%)	
Information provided	**Before 1754**	**After 1754**
Wife's Christian name	50%	60%
Wife's Christian *and* maiden names, *and* date of marriage	61%	67%
Wife's Christian name, *and* date *and* place of marriage	77%	91%
Wife's Christian *and* maiden names, *and* date *and* place of marriage	78%	96%

Table 6.1 Bradford-on-Avon settlement examinations (see p. 142)

For the genealogist hoping to ascertain the likelihood of ancestors marrying in any given place, what is also interesting about Bradford-on-Avon is the fact that it had the highest proportion of couples who married in a different county. In part this was down to the nature of the sample: consisting of couples being examined by the parish authorities as to their place of settlement, whether on account of their poverty or recent arrival, it naturally included many non-Wiltshire couples. But it was also down to the fact that many of the settlement examinations explicitly recorded where the couple had married. *Without* such evidence, the historian looking for the marriage of a couple resident in Bradford-on-Avon might discount a match in London; *with* such evidence, otherwise speculative marriages can be confirmed. Had such evidence been available for the other groups, it might have been possible to confirm various matches that had been traced further afield, and to bring the total traced up to 100%.

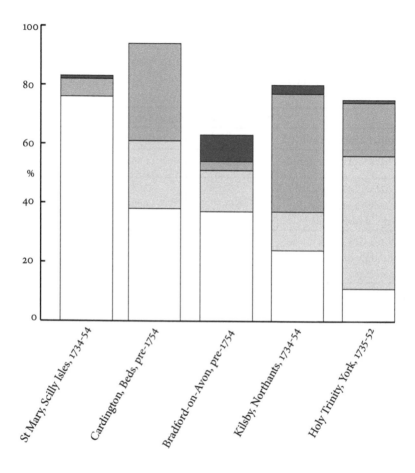

marriages
traced to...

■ different
county

▨ same
county

▧ adjacent
parish

□ same parish

Fig. 6.2 The proportions and relative
locations of marriages traced for couples
living in any given parish vary dramatically,
depending on its geography and other factors
(see p. 142)

The Fleet

The one marriage in the Bradford-on-Avon settlement examinations that took place in London is notable for another reason, for it took place in the Fleet prison (as did many other marriages in the first half of the eighteenth century). Legislation in the late 1690s had pushed 'clandestine' marriages out of churches and chapels and into more lawless places such as the narrow streets surrounding the Fleet prison. Known as the 'Rules of the Fleet', this was the area within which those imprisoned for debt were permitted to reside. The sudden increase in the popularity of the Fleet as a place to marry was not because the Rules were exempt from the law, but because any clergyman imprisoned there had little to lose, and much to gain, from celebrating marriages in defiance of the canon law.

Staggering numbers of marriages were celebrated within the Rules of the Fleet over the next few decades. A careful analysis of the Fleet marriage registers has led the historian Roger Lee Brown to estimate that by 1740 over 6,600 marriages were being celebrated there each year, which would account for more than half of all marriages in London (but not, it should be noted, more than half of all Londoners' marriages, since the registers record individuals from all over the country marrying in the Fleet).

The reasons that have been put forward for the popularity of the Fleet as a marriage venue are many and various: recent immigrants to London not having any affiliation to a particular parish, sailors on leave wanting to marry quickly, apprentices wishing to marry quietly, pregnant brides wishing to marry both quickly and quietly. All of these may have played a role. But those reasons also illustrate just how important marriage was to the society of the time. And the very popularity of the Fleet—attested by the 545 notebooks and 290 registers and indexes that survive—also drives home to us that there can be no truth in the idea that it was possible to marry by a simple exchange of consent. After all, why would anyone travel to a prison to pay to be married by an imprisoned clergyman if the same effect could be achieved by exchanging vows in the comfort of one's own home?

The vast number of clandestine marriages celebrated in the Fleet, and the fact that clergymen there were less than scrupulous about who they married, was the reason why Parliament was eventually galvanized into action. Lord Hardwicke's Clandestine Marriages Act of 1753 tightened up the rules on how marriages could be celebrated. But what impact did his Act have on where marriages *could* be celebrated, and where marriages were *in fact* celebrated?

FROM MARCH 25TH, 1754 TO JUNE 30TH, 1837

The 1753 Act directed that marriages should take place in the church of the parish where at least one of the parties was resident. But it also stipulated that no marriage could be challenged at a later date on the basis that neither of the parties had been resident in the parish in question: the requirement as to residence was directory, not mandatory. Nonetheless, it had a profound effect on where couples married. Across London, the removal of the Fleet prison as a marriage venue meant that many parishes saw a dramatic increase in the number of marriages (see Table 6.2). At St Giles in the Fields, for example, the number of marriages celebrated between 1754 and 1760 was almost quadruple what it had been between 1747 and 1753.

Parish	Marriages 1747-53	Marriages 1754-60	Change
St Clement Danes	331	770	+133%
Clerkenwell St James	311	544	+75%
St George Bloomsbury	175	352	+101%
St Giles in the Fields	231	1,167	+396%
St James Westminster	615	2,172	+253%
St Martin in the Fields	752	1,724	+129%
St Mary le Bone	216	659	+205%

Table 6.2 London marriages before and after the Clandestine Marriages Act (source: Lambeth Palace Library, *Fulham Papers*, Terrick 6, fols. 2-4)

Outside London, by contrast, some parishes saw an increase and some a fall in the wake of the 1753 Act, but this simply reflected the fact that the provinces had not had the same facilities for celebrating marriages clandestinely as had been available in London. Rural clandestinity had tended to involve marriages being celebrated in the 'wrong' church—i.e. in a parish where the parties were not resident—rather than in no church. As a result of the Act, any provincial parish which had previously attracted a high number of couples—whether because of cost, convenience, or other factors—experienced a fall in the number of marriages after the Act, as couples dutifully complied with the residential requirements. But if one examines the numbers marrying across a large number of parishes, the gains and losses of individual parishes evened out.

Fig. 6.3 (p. 149) illustrates this by showing the breakdown of marriages across Northamptonshire in the period immediately before and after the implementation of the 1753 Act. Three points are worthy of note: first, the general consistency in the number of marriages celebrated across the county before and after the Act; secondly, the dramatic impact on where couples married from 1754 onwards, with virtually all couples marrying in the parish where at least one of them was resident; and, thirdly, the equally dramatic improvement in the quality of recording, with most marriage registers recording both the bride and groom's parish of residence.

In the wake of the 1753 Act, the preference for the bride's parish became slightly more marked, with just over a third of all Northamptonshire marriages taking place in the parish where she lived, more than six times the number of marriages taking place in the groom's parish. The remaining 60% of marriages took place in the parish where both were resident.

The impact of the 1753 Act was particularly marked in Kilsby, as a comparison (Fig. 6.4, p. 149) of those bringing their children to be baptized before and after it illustrates. A subsequent fall, between 1800 and 1837, in the proportion of couples who married in Kilsby and went on to have children there was linked to a change in its population in this period rather than reduced compliance with the letter of the law. Of the 25% who married outside the county, over half (13.5%) married, as one might expect, in nearby Warwickshire, and a further 6.1% in Leicestershire, whose border was not far distant. But 5.4% married as far afield as Staffordshire, Lancashire and London, reflecting not just improved facilities for travel but also the influx of workers into Kilsby to work on the construction of the railway. Yet despite the overall pattern of conformity, there were of course some couples who sought to escape the requirements of the 1753 Act altogether and went out of the jurisdiction in order to marry.

Q. *Judging from the age of their oldest child, my ancestors must have married shortly after the 1753 Act came into force, but I have been unable to trace a marriage for them. Might they have eloped to Gretna Green?*

A. Gretna is probably the least likely place for an English couple to marry in the 1750s, for the simple reason that it was not until improvements to the toll roads were made in the 1770s that the hitherto obscure village of Graitney began to attract attention as a place to marry. But it was not unknown for couples to leave the jurisdiction in order to escape the effect of the 1753 Act, either to other destinations in Scotland (such as Coldstream) or perhaps to the Channel Islands.

FROM JULY 1ST, 1837

England under Queen Victoria was an increasingly mobile society, not least because of the coming of railways and steamships, and this was reflected in where couples married (although elopements to Scotland were effectively eliminated by legislation in 1856, which required three weeks' residence before a marriage could be celebrated there). Again, it is useful for the family historian to know the relative proportions of couples marrying locally and farther afield, in order to evaluate the likelihood of any particular possible match being correct.

The first point to stress is that despite the greater opportunities for travel, most couples did not travel particularly far in order to marry. The results for three contrasting communities—rural Kilsby, the Hertfordshire town of Great Berkhamsted, and the somewhat insalubrious suburb of Neithrop in the Oxfordshire town of Banbury—illustrate that most marriages will be found within a relatively short distance, even after 1837 (Fig. 6.5, p. 152). Having traced the marriages for those listed in the 1851 census for each community, the proportion of couples marrying after July 1st, 1837 who who had done so in the

148

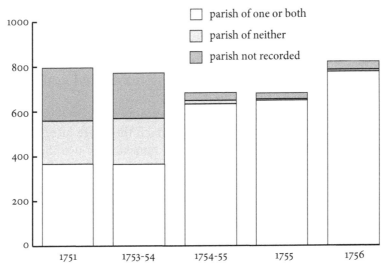

Fig. 6.3 Where Northamptonshire couples married, 1751-56 (see p. 147)

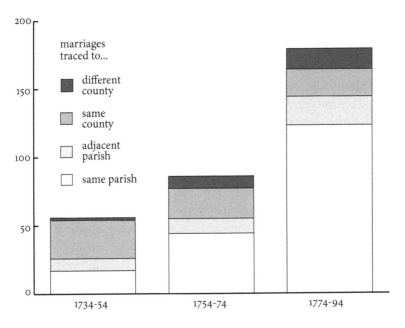

Fig. 6.4 Marriages of Kilsby residents, 1734-1794 (see p. 147)

registration district[1] where they were resident ranged from one half to two thirds of the samples (52% in Great Berkhamsted, 60.5% in Kilsby, 65% in Neithrop). A further case-study of the densely populated industrial town of Salford, Lancashire, in 1901 revealed a similar percentage: 64% of the 1,035 couples listed had married in Salford registration district (Fig. 6.5, p. 151).

If we add in those couples who married outside their registration district but within the *same county* in which they were recorded in the census, the total proportions traced ranged from two thirds to nine tenths (65% for Great Berkhamsted, 73% for Neithrop, 81.5% for Kilsby and 91% for Salford). This means that the proportion of marriages taking place *outside the county* ranged from 9% (Salford, 1901) to 35% (Great Berkhamsted, 1851).

When we look in detail at those marriages that took place outside the county, there are two further key messages for the family historian. Anyone who has searched for an ancestor's marriage will know that finding a match is one thing, confirming it quite another, and the data from Great Berkhamsted illustrate the fact that matches should not be discounted simply because the marriage in question took place in an unexpected location. In over half of the marriages outside Hertfordshire, census details for the husband, wife or children showed that at least one of them had been born in the county where the marriage took place. But for a not-insignificant 44% of the marriages that took place outside Hertfordshire (or 15% of all the marriages in the sample), the place of marriage was different from the county/-ies of birth of husband, wife and children.

Some were families who had clearly moved around a lot; others appear to have travelled from Great Berkhamsted to some London parish for the express purpose of marrying (their home parish being noted in the register). Other matches were at first sight unlikely but were confirmed by other census details (for example where it was possible to infer the wife's maiden name from other members of the household, or where the names were unique). The high proportion (35%) of marriages taking place outside the county was no doubt a result of Great Berkhamsted's proximity to London, but the disparity

1 For the purpose of registering all marriages, civil and religious, parishes were
  aggregated into larger 'registration districts' by the Marriage Act 1836.

between the parties' places of birth and the location of the marriage was not unique to Great Berkhamsted: of the handful of Kilsby couples who had married outside Northamptonshire, the place of marriage matched the counties of birth in less than one quarter of cases. (Of course, a marriage that takes place outside the parties' county of residence might still be relatively close in terms of the distance travelled: Kilsby, Neithrop and Great Berkhamsted are all close to county borders, and a significant proportion of marriages took place in the adjacent county.)

But within each sample there was a core of around 10% of marriages that had taken place significantly further afield. One striking example of mobility was that of the Wesleyan minister from Cornwall, who married in Wiltshire and whose children were born in the Caribbean before moving to Neithrop! Similarly, while most of the Salford marriages were traced within the county, the distances travelled by the 9% who had married outside Lancashire were quite considerable, with weddings having taken place as far afield as Cardiff, County Durham, Glasgow, Medway, Plymouth, and even Toronto.

If anything, these figures underestimate the proportion of marriages that took place further afield. Like all family historians, I have a list of 'possible but unverifiable' matches, and another of those which are untraceable because the marriage, to judge from other census details, took place overseas in a location that does not have easily accessible registers. But this last group, it should be noted, accounts for a relatively small proportion of the total. In all, marriages were found for 95% of the Neithrop sample and 96% of Great Berkhamsted. Even in turn-of-the-century Salford, thought of as a place where unmarried cohabitation was common, matches could be confirmed for 94% of the sample. And for Kilsby it proved possible to trace marriages for 100% of the couples resident there at the time of the 1851 census, with the information amassed on baptisms and marriages over the previous 150 years proving crucial in confirming the last few.

In summary

While the precise proportion of marriages that can be traced to a couple's home registration district or county will vary according to the location, the search for any given ancestor in this period will on

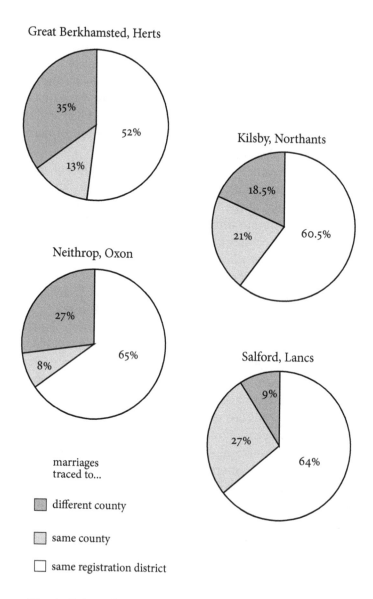

Fig. 6.5 Relative locations of marriages after 1837 (see p. 148)

balance remain quite a local matter, but will often (in around one tenth of cases) be a national one, while in perhaps 1% or so of cases the search will need to be global.

CASE-STUDY: FROM TYNESIDE TO NEW YORK

The 1841 census records 3-year-old Annie Noble living with 30-year-old Isabella Noble. A single mother, perhaps? In fact, Isabella was Annie's aunt, and her parents James and Anne (née Watson) were absent. But no record of James' and Anne's marriage could be traced locally, and the fact that Anne was born in Wiltshire, James in London, and Annie on Tyneside, meant that it could feasibly have taken place anywhere in the country.

The marriage was only traced when the *Christian Intelligencer of the Reformed Dutch Church of New York* was digitised and made available online. They had married in Manhattan in 1833, in an Anglican church, at a time when there was no requirement for records to be kept. It was simply good fortune that the *Christian Intelligencer* had included this particular event in its reporting of marriages within other denominations.

Now it was certain that James and Anne had both been in New York in 1833, the passenger lists of ships arriving there did indeed record Anne's arrival, while the newspapers' *Shipping Intelligence* columns also confirmed that James Noble (a sea-captain) had reached New York a short time before on the *Miriam & Jane*.

MARRIAGE ACROSS THE GLOBE

Those family historians who have discovered that their English and Welsh ancestors married overseas may well have questions about the validity of such marriages. It would require several hefty volumes to give a comprehensive account of the relevant laws that applied across the globe at different times, and instead a brief sketch of how English law approached the question of whether overseas marriages were valid will suffice to show what the key issues were and alert the family historian to questions that might need further investigation.

The law of the place where the marriage was celebrated

The general rule in English law that the validity of a marriage was to be tested by the law of the place where it was celebrated (the *lex loci*) was well established by 1800. Perhaps unsurprisingly, all the early cases on this point involved marriages across the Channel, in Europe. Such jurisdictions' requirements for a valid marriage were familiar, being founded on Christian ecclesiastical rules, and were usually more stringent than those required in England and Wales even after the 1753 Act. The one important qualification to this general rule was that an individual's capacity to marry was governed by the law of the country where he or she was domiciled. This meant that people from England and Wales could not, by going overseas, escape restrictions on whom they could marry (see p. 65).

Places where English law applied

But the law of the place where a marriage was celebrated might in certain circumstances be English law, even when it was celebrated overseas: embassies, merchant ships, territorial concessions and 'factories' (trading settlements) were all regarded as part of their home nation. Since none of the legislation passed from 1753 onwards applied outside England and Wales, the only requirement for a marriage in such locations was for it to be celebrated by an Anglican clergyman.

New difficulties arose as the British began to spread across the globe as conquerors, rather than visitors, and into areas that did not have the sort of infrastructure that was necessary for the formal celebration of weddings. In some colonies marriage was governed by statute from an early stage, and what was required for a valid marriage was clear. In other places, by contrast, where the tentacles of the Empire had spread out in advance of any formal settlement, thornier questions arose. Particularly difficult was the issue of how members of the army should marry (for example if a soldier married the widow of a comrade), since advancing troops could hardly be expected to comply with the regulations of the nation that they were attempting to overcome, but at the same time the disputed territory could not be regarded as being under British rule.

Cases from the late eighteenth century and the first decade of the nineteenth show the courts struggling with these questions, but then in 1811, with admirable timing, a simple solution presented itself. In that year, it was (mistakenly) decided by a church court in London that, prior to the 1753 Marriage Act, English law had allowed marriages to be celebrated by a simple exchange of consent, rather than (as was actually the case) needing to be celebrated before an Anglican clergyman (see p. 25). At around the same time it was held that English common law (i.e., the canon law that had applied before Parliament put marriage on a statutory basis in 1753) would apply in those colonies that had not passed specific laws regulating marriage, or where a soldier in an advancing army had married. Putting the two developments together meant that those wishing to marry in such situations would not need to find an Anglican clergyman to conduct the ceremony. This new option become known as a common-law marriage. In other words, the option of common-law marriage was invented when it was convenient to do so, when English law was dealing with the marriages of British citizens in foreign parts. Had missionaries to the colonies all been ordained Anglican clergymen, the necessity might not have arisen, but many were dissenters. Deciding that all that was needed for a valid marriage was an exchange of consent sidestepped the question of who had authority to conduct a marriage, even if, in practice, most marriages continued to be celebrated before a religious functionary. It also meant that any earlier marriages whose validity was disputed could be upheld even if they had not been celebrated by an Anglican clergyman, on the new (if mistaken) basis that his presence had never been necessary.[2]

The desire to uphold marriages wherever possible, combined with a certain degree of imperial arrogance, even led to English common

2 The 1844 House of Lords ruling in *R v Millis*, correctly holding that English law had always required an Anglican clergyman, briefly looked as if might pose problems for this convenient solution. The courts however soon found a way around *Millis*, deciding that colonists only took so much of the law of England with them as was capable of being applied to their particular location. Where there was no established church, the requirement of an Anglican minister could therefore be dispensed with. The case-law on these points becomes complex indeed, and interested readers are referred to '*R v Millis* Reconsidered: Binding Contracts and Bigamous Marriages' (2008) 28 *Legal Studies* 337.

law being applied to countries that were not actually under British rule at all. The courts held that if there were insuperable objections to the parties marrying according to the local law, then English common law would be applied. More practically, the need to rely on the common law to validate a ceremony that had not complied with the local law was reduced by the passage of the Consular Marriages Act 1849, allowing marriages to be celebrated before any British Consul (and retrospectively validating all such previous marriages). Later legislation extended the range of people who could conduct such marriages. For the family historian, one major advantage of a consular marriage was that the 1849 Act directed that copies of the registers be sent to England (the originals are now kept in the National Archives). By contrast, it has never been a requirement that couples marrying overseas re-register their marriage upon returning home, which makes tracing some overseas marriages a matter of searching for a needle in a very big haystack.

Marriages on board ships

What of the common idea that it is possible for a ship's captain to conduct a marriage? There is some truth in this, since the Foreign Marriages Act 1892 explicitly dealt with the possibility of a marriage being solemnized on a man-of-war in the presence of one of its commanding officers, and the Merchant Shipping Act 1894 made provision for weddings on merchant ships to be registered (but without explaining how the actual ceremony should be carried out).

Whether marriage aboard ship was possible before 1892 is unclear: since the statutory law on marriage applied only to England and Wales, marriages on British ships elsewhere in the world remained governed by the law as it had stood before March 25th, 1753. This meant that, before the 1811 case of *Dalrymple*, it would have been assumed that a clergyman had to be present on board to conduct the ceremony, while after *Dalrymple* it would have been assumed that this was not (and never had been) necessary. Any subsequent doubts over the validity of marriages that might have been celebrated by ships' captains were done away with by the retrospective provisions of the Consular Marriages Act 1849. Further retrospective legislation was passed in 1879: the Confirmation of Marriages on Her Majesty's

Ships Act noted that officers had allowed marriages to be solemnized on board their ships, acknowledged that there were doubts about their validity, and declared them to be valid, but made no provision for similar marriages in the future.

For the family historian, the point to note is that the combination of retrospective and prospective legislation means that the validity of a marriage would only be in doubt if it were celebrated between 1879 and 1892 and without an Anglican clergyman presiding. There are few precedents to offer any guidance on what the status of a wedding would be if celebrated by the ship's captain between these dates: the only clear case (which came before the Irish courts in 1860, and in which a marriage celebrated by a ship's commanding officer was declared void) would not be binding on the English courts.

In short, although there is of course no guarantee that any given marriage celebrated overseas was valid, the family historian must bear in mind that English law did all that lay within its power to prevent marriages being invalidated for a failure to comply with formal requirements, wherever in the world they were celebrated.

A FINAL THOUGHT...

If the evidence in this chapter seems complex, spare a thought for future generations of genealogists. Since 1995 it has been possible for couples to marry in a civil ceremony outside their area of residence, and indeed in a far wider range of places, such as castles, stately homes and even the occasional supermarket. And today's couples are far more likely than even their recent predecessors to jet off to the far side of the world to tie the knot. It has been estimated that in 2009 90,000 individuals travelled abroad from England and Wales to marry, and, since these overseas marriages do not need to be re-registered when the couple return to this country, our descendants attempting to trace marriages in the late twentieth and early twenty-first centuries may find themselves baffled.

FURTHER READING

For further information on the cohort studies in this chapter
Probert R. and D'Arcy-Brown, L. 'The Impact of the Clandestine Marriages Act: Three Case-studies in Conformity' (2008) 23 *Continuity and Change* 309-330

Probert, R. and D'Arcy-Brown, L. 'The Clandestine Marriages Act of 1753 in Action: Investigating a Contemporary Complaint' (2009) 83 *Local Population Studies* 66

On marriages in the Fleet
Brown, RL. 'The Rise and Fall of the Fleet Marriages' in Outhwaite (ed), *Marriage and Society* (Europa Publications, 1981)

Brown, RL. *A History of the Fleet Prison, London* (Mellen Press, 1996)

On the geography of marriage
Snell, KDM. 'English Rural Societies and Geographical Marital Endogamy, 1700-1837' (2002) 55 *Economic History Review* 262

On marriages overseas
Probert, R. '*R v Millis* Reconsidered: Binding Contracts and Bigamous Marriages' (2008) 28 *Legal Studies* 337

Get in Touch

warwick.ac.uk/marriagelawforgenealogists

I hope you have found this book useful and interesting.

As an academic researcher, I'm particularly interested in finding out whether my work has had an impact upon people's understanding of the topics it covers. I'd be very grateful if readers could visit my website (above) to answer some quick questions on this. The website also contains links to further reading, and more cohort studies will be added as my research progresses.

Many of the questions posed in this book come from family historians who have contacted me over the years, and I have deliberately focused on those issues that those tracing their family tree are most likely to encounter in their research. If you haven't found the answer to a particularly puzzling marriage in the preceding pages, please do contact me via my website and I will do my best to provide an answer. If your question concerns divorce, bigamy, or second marriages, you should find that the sister to this book—*Divorced, Bigamist, Bereaved?*—covers it.

If you would like to share any interesting or unexpected stories you have uncovered about how your ancestors married, I would also be delighted to hear from you (please remember though that I am unable to give legal advice on existing marriages!).

And if there any aspects of marriage law which you would like to see covered in more detail, please do let me know so that I can include these in future editions.

Acknowledgements

The research underpinning the conclusions of this book has entailed visiting numerous archives and libraries, and I would like to thank all the helpful staff at the National Archives, Bedfordshire and Luton Archives and Records Service, the Bodleian Library, the Borthwick Institute at York University, the British Library, Cambridge University Library, the Centre for Buckinghamshire Studies, Carlisle Record Office, Chester Record Office, the Family Records Centre, the Guildhall Library, the Institute for Historical Research, Lambeth Palace Library, the University of London Library, the London Metropolitan Archives, Gloucestershire Record Office, Hertfordshire Archives and Local Studies, Kendal Record Office, the Record Office for Leicestershire, Leicester and Rutland, Lichfield Record Office, Northamptonshire Record Office, Oxfordshire History Centre, the Centre for Oxfordshire Studies, the Quaker Library, the Society of Genealogists' Library, Somerset Record Office, Warwickshire County Record Office, Dr Williams's Library, and Wiltshire and Swindon Record Office.

Special thanks also go to Mrs Morris for her kind assistance in proofreading. Finally, I would like to thank all of the family historians who have shared their stories and questions with me over the years.